# AMY WINEHOUSE

## A Losing Game

D1042657

# AMY WINEHOUSE

## A Losing Game

*Mick O'Shea*

Plexus, London

# CONTENTS

# Amy Winehouse
# A Losing Game

'Amy was about one thing and that was love,
her whole life was devoted to her family and her friends.'
– Mitch Winehouse

For those tourists with an eye for style, aside from Carnaby Street, Madame Tussauds and the London Eye, a visit to London will almost certainly include a trip to Camden Town, and the celebrated labyrinthine market that made it the counter-cultural capital of the world. People come in their droves to rummage through vintage clothes, get a ring through their nose, or stop off for food before popping into the World's End pub for a pint.

Camden is also renowned for its musical heritage. It's where the Clash staged their early rehearsals, and Sid Vicious played his one and only UK solo show at the Electric Circus. Madness sang for their supper at the Dublin Castle, and Noel and Liam held court at the Good Mixer on Inverness Street. And in recent years, of course, it's been home to the Camden Crawl, a two-day bohemian celebration during which bands are happy to play on the street. Though its pubs and clubs all eventually close, the party never really stops. And come the dawn, early morning traders can be seen exchanging pleasantries with those still coming down from the night before.

In that respect Saturday, 23 July 2011 would have been much like any other Saturday, and few if any of the shoppers walking the streets that afternoon would have given much thought to the wailing siren of the ambulance as it turned off Camden Road onto Murray Street. The well-heeled residents of the lavish Victorian townhouses that line Camden Square had become accustomed to seeing scooter-mounted paparazzi circling the area, in the hope of snapping their quarry popping out to pick up a bottle of milk or performing some equally mundane chore, but they knew something untoward was occurring when the ambulance screeched to a halt

*Amy Winehouse photographed at London's Somerset House before performing*
*at the venue in July 2007, a few weeks before her first major drugs overdose.*

*I fought the law: Amy Winehouse outside Westminster Magistrates Court on 23 July 2009, when she was on trial for assaulting a fan, a charge she was acquitted of.*

outside the home of the beehived young singer who'd thrown the odd noisy party since moving in a couple of months earlier. Those who knew the singer by name, and were aware of her reputation, would perhaps have been more concerned. And any lingering hopes that it might not be too late disappeared into the early evening air as paramedics emerged unruffled from the house a few minutes later, and the attendant police officers began cordoning off the square.

A few hundred yards away – now that the tourists were gone, and the traders were packed up for the day – Camden's back streets were gradually filling up with revellers as another Saturday night got underway. But ever so slowly, the joyful mood began to sour as hushed whispers filtered across the night air; whispers that would soon spread around the globe. Amy Winehouse was dead.

Though the rumours were confirmed in that most chilling fashion, when three stern-faced, besuited gentlemen emerged with Amy's body respectfully hidden away within a maroon body-bag and then loaded into the back of a private ambulance, as when most out-of-the-blue tragedies occur, the fragile human psyche is unable to

*Amy takes a break during her performance for the 2008 Grammy Awards, which was broadcast from London via satellite after she was denied a US visa.*

process the information, and it's only when we see the stark banner headlines the following morning that we begin to accept the reality.

I have to admit that the news of Amy's death came as more of a shock than a surprise; the shock simply being that she hadn't shuffled off her mortal coil earlier than she did. After all, having watched my own childhood rebel, ex-Sex Pistol Sid Vicious, wending his way to oblivion some thirty-odd years earlier, the telltale signs were there for all to see. And even if I'd had no interest in either Amy or her music, her trashy transition from cutesy girl-next-door to the bastard offspring of Jake Blues and Ronnie Spector was for a time an unavoidable fixture in the national press, all-too-well-documented in magazines like *OK!*, *Now*, *Heat* and *Hello*.

Since starting this book I've come to think of Amy's tale as an alternate spin on *The Picture of Dorian Grey*. Whereas Oscar Wilde's fictional anti-hero kept his youth and beauty while his canvas-borne image suffered the ravages of his wicked ways, it was Amy's voice that remained untouchably beautiful while, with each tabloid exposé, the once-innocent girl was slowly morphine-ing into a wasted shadow of her former self; a haunted caricature with a beehive and a penchant for 'Jolly Jack Tar' tattoos.

> **'Too fragile, too beautiful, too big a talent for this world.'**
> – A note left outside Amy Winehouse's house by a fan

Like Etta and Ella, and those other doomed divas of yesteryear, Amy burst onto the music scene chock full of soul; her jazz-bejewelled debut album, *Frank*, a joy to behold. But it was while the world was still marvelling over her voice that a new boyfriend entered her world; his untimely arrival heralded, in true Amy fashion, by a new tattoo bearing her lover's name. Within no time at all, lurid tales of the star-crossed lovers engaging in their nocturnal binges began to take up more column inches than Amy's talent. And that was perhaps the first telling indication that she wouldn't be adding many more candles to her birthday cake. With hindsight, we now know that Amy was simply doing with Blake Fielder-Civil what she did in every other facet of her life – giving herself whole. Not so much attention to detail, but rather *addiction* to detail, for there was never any room for half-measures in Amy's world – regardless of what was in the bottle.

As we've seen from the outpourings of grief from her millions of fans around the globe, the nerve is still too raw for them to contemplate a future without Amy's music to guide the way. But whether she sashayed, staggered, or was dragged kicking and screaming up to the celestial rehab in the sky, Amy's legacy will undoubtedly live on.

**Mick O'Shea**

*Smile and the world smiles with you: Amy onstage at the Isle of Wight Festival at the height of* Back to Black's *success, June 2007.*

# 1. The Girl from Southgate

**'I don't think your ability to fight has anything to do with how big you are. It's to do with how much anger is in you.'**

From the moment Amy Jade Winehouse came wailing into the world at Chase Farm Hospital in Enfield, north London, during the early hours of 14 September 1983, her world was filled with music. Her mum Janis and larger-than-life paternal grandma Cynthia – or 'Cynthie' as she was affectionately known by all who knew her – hummed soft lullabies in the maternity ward. Her dad Mitchell, who himself possesses a passable singing voice, serenaded her to sleep with Frank Sinatra songs in her cot at the family home, which at the time was a nondescript two-bedroom flat in the predominantly Jewish suburb of Southgate, north London. Though the flat could easily accommodate the new arrival, before Amy had learnt to crawl the Winehouses moved into a three-bedroom, semi-detached 1930s house situated upon a gently sloping rise in the area's Chase Side, in what had once been the Enfield Chase royal hunting reserve.

Ol' Blue Eyes would also play an important part in forming the unbreakable father-daughter bond that would endure throughout Amy's life. When the time came for Amy to go to school, Mitch, as Mr Winehouse prefers to be called, was working as a taxi driver, and the two of them would belt out songs for swinging lovers during the car ride to the school gates.

By September 1983, Britain had well and truly emerged from the financial mire that had gripped the country in the immediate wake of the Conservatives' return to power four years earlier. Mitch Winehouse was doing very nicely working as a double-glazing salesman, while Janis, a pharmacy technician, had recently completed an Open University science degree, and would later go on to study at the School of Pharmacy, housed within the University of London.

*Amy aged nineteen in February 2003, posing in a Camden launderette at one of her first photo shoots.*

'Amy was a beautiful child, always busy, always curious, always cheery,' Janis would tell the *Daily Mail*'s Alun Palmer in 2007. But even at such a tender age, Amy's now-legendary wanton recklessness was becoming evident. 'As a toddler in her pram she once nearly choked on Cellophane. Another time she went missing in the park. But she's tough like me, I see that as my gift to her.' She also apparently thought it fun to go AWOL during shopping excursions to Brent Cross Shopping Centre, while another favourite jape was feigning choking whilst eating her meals. Of course, attention-seeking is a mischievous part of any child's make-up, just as keeping a watchful eye on their offspring comes as second nature to mothers everywhere. And though Janis and Mitch already had a wealth of experience from nurturing their firstborn (Amy's older brother, Alex, born in 1979), Janis suspected early on that Amy would need more watching than most. 'She's reckless, very determined, and if she wants to do something she will just do it,' she told Palmer. 'No one can stop her once she's made her mind up, but she never stops to think of the consequences.'

Southgate, which primarily lies within the borough of Enfield, is famed for its beautiful landscaped parks, and when she wasn't amusing her classmates and driving her teachers to distraction at Osidge Primary School in Barnet by singing in class, or learning the basics of Judaism at Cheder classes on Sundays, tomboy Amy would be off climbing trees and skimming her knees. 'I was born in Southgate in north London, and I lived down the road from my nan,' Amy told *Access All Areas* in 2006. 'I was a good girl, I really liked school. I really liked learning. I wasn't really a trouble-maker you know . . . not more than other kids, you know what I mean!'

Cuts and bruises are part and parcel of any child's world, but no amount of Germolene was going to salve the pain when Mitch and Janis broke the news that they were to separate. By this time the family were living in a cosy, three-bedroom Victorian terraced house a short walk further up the rise on Osidge Lane, but following the split Amy and Alex went to live in East Finchley with Janis.

Though nary a cross word had passed between Mitch and Janis during some fourteen years of wedlock, the marriage was inevitably doomed to failure. One of the reasons was the nature of Mitch's high-pressure sales job, as he was constantly away from home. Another, less palatable and unpardonable reason – in Janis's eyes at least – was his long-standing affair with a woman called Jane (whom Mitch would subsequently marry) coming to light. 'I think Mitchell would have liked to have both of us, but I wasn't happy to do that,' was how Janis eventually rationalised these events. 'I have looked back and thought how could we have done things differently,' Mitch said in February 2010. 'Maybe if I had stayed with Amy's mum – I was not unhappy with her but I wanted to be with Jane. What would that have done to me? Maybe it would have made the situation worse. Maybe if I had been firmer with Amy. Maybe I was too firm. We did the best that we could in our own limited way. We encouraged our children, we didn't bully them and we didn't hit them . . . maybe we could have done better, I don't know.'

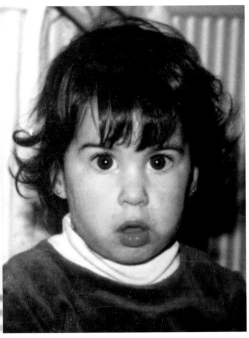 

*Daddy's girl: Family photographs of Amy aged two (in 1985, left), and five (in 1988, right). 'Amy was a beautiful child, always busy, always curious, always cheery,' said her mother Janis.*

Outwardly, Amy gave little away, and though she saw as much of her dad as his job allowed, the emotional turmoil of the family break-up left her devastated. It would be many years down the line before Mitch would admit – as much to himself, as anyone else – that the split left his daughter with wounds that may have scabbed over, but which never really healed. 'Perhaps deep down she felt her parents were splitting up, she could not rely on them to stay together and that it was about time she learned to look after herself,' Mitch told the *Mirror* in July 2007. 'I thought Amy was over it pretty quickly – in fact it felt at the time [that] Amy felt no effect at all. Maybe she could not articulate it in words, but she certainly did it with music.'

In later years Amy would play down the effect that Mitch's infidelity had on her, claiming, 'People like to have sex with people. I don't begrudge my dad just because he has a penis.' But Janis, who had the unenviable job of picking up the disjointed pieces, knew that the cute, doe-eyed girl staring out from the family photo album, sporting an array of theatrical accessories such as hula skirts and Mickey Mouse ears, was gone forever.

♪ ♪ ♪

As with every other teenage girl up and down the country, pop music featured heavily in Amy's life. 'You know how you either grow up in a Michael Jackson house or a

Prince house?' Amy said in the *Guardian* in 2004. 'For me it was Michael Jackson. I could never decide whether I wanted to be Michael Jackson or marry him. I don't care what people say about him now because he's a fucking genius. That's it – the end! He was robbed of his childhood, which is why he surrounds himself with children. When you're around kids you can be a little kid yourself and pretend that life is magic and you don't have to be one of those sweaty people going to work every day. I completely see what he's doing.'

Though Jacko was her pop star pin-up, Amy was fast developing a love of jazz and soul, and after school she'd head round to Cynthie's and sing along to the old girl's sizeable record collection. Cynthie, whose youthful outlook and jazz-imbued joie de vivre belied her advancing years, would take on a pivotal role in Amy's life. Her own love of jazz came from her brother Mort being a professional horn player, while she herself had at one time been romantically involved with the renowned jazz saxophonist, and jazz club owner, Ronnie Scott.

Chain-smoking Cynthie would succumb to lung cancer in 2006, and the following January Amy paid tribute to her nan by saying that if her idol Frank Sinatra had encountered Cynthie before he met Hollywood actress Ava Gardner (once considered to be one of the most beautiful women of her day), then she'd be 'lounge royalty'.

> **'I could never decide whether I wanted to be Michael Jackson or marry him.' – Amy Winehouse**

Indeed, some of Amy's biographers have pointed to Cynthie – upon realising that her granddaughter possessed a singing voice capable of matching those emanating from the turntable – as being the one responsible for suggesting Amy abandon her studies at the Ashmole Secondary School and instead enrol at the prestigious Sylvia Young Theatre School in Marylebone. Others claim, however, that it was simply Amy's first overt display of her self-nurtured independent streak coming to the fore. Either way, she was given a scholarship. 'All the teachers at school hated me. And every school I've ever been to has put me on report,' Amy told *Times Online* in October 2003. 'They'd write how you were in a lesson – with me, it was like, "Came into the classroom with a safety pin in her ear. Didn't want to remove it. And then cried in front of everyone."'

Though Janis had supposedly played no part in her daughter getting the scholarship, it was around this time – the summer of 1995 – that she first became aware of Amy's creative bent. She and Cynthie had whisked Amy and Alex off to Cyprus on holiday. Each week the hotel staged a talent show for the children, and though Janis neglects to say whether Amy collected a prize for her efforts, this was the eureka moment when she realised her daughter had 'something really special'. Yet whilst reminiscing about Amy's childhood, she confessed that she would've preferred her daughter to continue her education at the Ashmole School.

The Sylvia Young Theatre School was originally established on Drury Lane in 1981, but when Amy became a pupil it was located in larger premises on Rossmore Road in Marylebone. In its thirty-year history to date, the SYTS has nurtured the talents of many an *EastEnders* actor, as well as singers such as Bow Wow Wow's Annabella Lwin, All Saints siblings Natalie and Nicole Appleton, Spice Girl Emma Bunton, and the 2006 *X Factor* sensation Leona Lewis.

Singing cheesy show tunes with her more dutiful classmates was anathema to a free-spirited firebrand like Amy. Though as bright and intelligent as her peers, she was equally loath to apply herself to the prerequisite academic studies. 'The thing about stage school is that it doesn't necessarily prepare you or train you for your skills,' Amy told *Music OMH* in 2007. 'They prepare you as a person and are good for building character.'

When it came to singing soulful jazz numbers, however, Amy was in a class of her own. Her talent was such that she was moved up a year, but she was still bored and easily distracted in the classroom. A salvation of sorts came when Cynthie presented her with her first acoustic guitar, and from then on she diligently set about mastering open chords so that she might put her thoughts and observations into words and formulate her own songs. 'My brother taught himself [the guitar],' Amy told *Music OMH* shortly after receiving her first Ivor Novello nomination in 2004. 'So I took inspiration for teaching myself from him and he showed me a couple of things.'

She would subsequently perform these songs either at family parties and bar mitzvahs, or for her small circle of friends, and while it was hardly the O2 Arena, it did at least provide Amy with her first taste of performing in front of a live audience.

It was also whilst Amy was at the SYTS that she made her television debut, when she and some of her fellow pupils made a cameo appearance in the second episode of the final series of *The Fast Show*, BBC Two's zany Friday-night comedy sketch show, which ran for three series and made household names of Paul Whitehouse, Mark Williams, and Caroline 'Mrs Merton' Aherne. The sketch, which was first aired on Friday, 21 November 1997, was called 'Peasblossom'. And while it's very much a 'blink-and-you'll-miss-it' affair, Amy's credit is logged at imdb.com.

Sylvia Young was astute enough to know that stardom beckoned for the wayward fifteen-year-old, but neither she nor her put upon staff could continue ignoring Amy's blatant disregard for the rules. She arrived late for lessons, chewed gum in class, and flouted the school's strict dress code by turning up with her nose pierced. 'I know life's about learnin',' Amy explained to journalist David Jenkins in 2004, 'but there's so many things you can't be told by someone who's old and past it.' The school, however, had a reputation to uphold, and Janis was summarily summoned to Sylvia Young's office and informed that it was best for all concerned if her daughter's three-year tenure at the school was brought to an end. Despite her defiant attitude, Amy later admitted to being devastated. 'They've got a reputation because they are the best,' she told journalist Paul du Noyer of the stage school. 'It's not a pop star factory, they channel your creativity and you learn to use it. That's what I did. For every precocious kid there were kids who really worked. They sent you out to work. Stage school is a job. You learn how to get the fuck on with it. I learned a lot of important things.'

Perhaps reluctant for people to think that she showed the door to one of the greatest singing talents the world has ever produced over something as trivial as a nose-stud, Sylvia Young has since refuted the claim that Amy was expelled from the school, and remains adamant that she left of her own free will. Janis, however, remembers the day well because it was the same day she had to take the family's ailing cat to the vet to be put to sleep. She would later joke that she should have had Amy put down and the cat moved on.

Sylvia Young had recommended a spell at a private, all-girls' school ('My dad was, "Why all girls? Are you sayin' she's a slut?"' Amy told David Jenkins), and Amy subsequently moved to the fee-paying Mount School in Mill Hill, north London. But as would be the case for any fifteen-year-old suddenly forced to switch schools at so late a stage in the game, friendships of any meaning were virtually impossible to forge. However, her enforced solitude paid dividends in her achieving the five GCSEs required to secure a place at the London School for Performing Arts and Technology in Croydon, south London – or 'the Brit School' as it's more colloquially known, part of its annual funding coming from monies raised at the Brit (British Record Industry Trust) Music Awards Ceremon. Amy's time there, however, would prove extremely brief. 'She simply dropped out,' Adrian Packer, one of Amy's teachers, recalled when Amy picked up the Brit Award for 'Best British Female Artist' in 2007. 'Teaching Amy was exciting but nerve-wracking. She was an artist from the age of sixteen, and wasn't exactly suited to being institutionalised.'

Having first opened its doors in 1991, the Brit School now boasts an impressive array of female singer-songwriters amongst its alumni. Leona Lewis, Katie Melua, Jessie J, Kate Nash, and Katy B, as well as Amy's fellow Grammy Award-winner Adele, have all passed through its hallowed portal. But as talented as each and every one of them surely are, none – with the exception of Adele – have come close to emulating Amy's extraordinary success.

♪♪♪

Out in the big world, Amy could finally unfurl her wings, but her aversion to being caged for any period of time meant she aimlessly drifted from one dead-end job to another. These included brief stints working in a fashion boutique, a tattoo parlour, and a low-rent body-piercing establishment, as well as more mundane office temping positions. 'I was the sort of secretary where it'd be, "Amy, make me a cup of tea." "No, fuck off,"' she said in a phone interview with *Popjustice* in 2008. 'You should call Ryman's [high-street stationary chain] for their catalogue. Hang on, are you taking the piss out of me? You fucker! Really? Call Ryman's. Or . . . Are you being serious?

Just go to another secretary and get her to order it. You *were* taking the piss, weren't you?' A rather more fulfilling – and enduring – role came in working as a showbiz journalist at the London offices of the World Entertainment News Network, the 24/7 global entertainment text and photo wire services provider, set up a decade or so earlier by her old school friend Juliette Ashby's father, Jonathan. 'Amy and I got to know each other years ago when we worked together at WENN,' ex-*Daily Star* columnist Charli Morgan wrote in *OK!* magazine in August 2011. 'Even after she'd left and started winning plaudits for her incredible voice, she would pop in on nightshifts, ever the sociable night owl, looking for company and someone to share a sugary tea and a gossip with.'

But of course, when Amy wasn't conjuring up good copy on Hollywood's current bright young things for her editor, she could more often than not be found belting out soul classics with a succession of jazz outfits on London's pub and club circuit. 'I think I started writing songs when I was fifteen or something . . . I just liked writing songs,'

> **'I think I started writing songs when I was fifteen or something . . . I just liked writing songs. I really didn't start knocking on management company doors or anything. I wrote some songs, started playing gigs. I just played pub gigs.'**
> **– Amy Winehouse**

Amy told *Access All Areas*. 'I really didn't start knocking on management company doors or anything. I wrote some songs, started playing gigs. I just played pub gigs. I had some songs and just did pub gigs. I'd go in with my Strat or something and just play pub gigs. I used to do gigs with a band called the Bolsha Band. It was cool because if they were playing they'd have their ramp there and I could go on before them, do a few songs . . . like just me . . . and then they'd do their set . . . I'd then go and do a couple of songs with them at the end of their set.'

To the casual observer, it might have seemed that Amy's dreams and aspirations were fading into the ether. But Janis and Cynthie weren't the only mother hens casting a watchful eye over Amy's development – or lack thereof. Sylvia Young had also been monitoring the situation, and she stepped in to arrange for Amy to audition with the National Youth Jazz Orchestra at the nearby Cockpit Theatre. Any preconceptions that the orchestra's bandleader, Bill Ashton, may have had on hearing Amy's faux-cockney 'norff Lahndan' accent melted away the moment Amy opened her mouth. It's hard to believe – given Amy's subsequent success – that her debut live performance was watched by just fifty or so jazz enthusiasts gathered in the nondescript bar of a hotel in northwest London.

According to Ashton, the NYJO's current chairman (who founded the orchestra back in 1965), Amy's debut came about simply because they didn't have a singer for one of their monthly Sunday lunchtime performances. Though she only learnt the names of the four songs she'd be expected to sing during Ashton's subsequent telephone call (one of which was the 1923 blues standard 'Nobody Knows You When You're Down and Out', first recorded by blues inveterate Bessie Smith), she learnt the lyrics on the Tube whilst making her way to the venue. As the recording shows, she performed them note and pitch perfect.

Another person who was astounded by Amy's professionalism at such a tender age was Annabel Williams, herself a professional jazz singer, who was acting as Amy's singing tutor that day. Though Amy appeared more interested in the cigarette she was smoking than what was being said to her during the practice session, Williams later reflected that 'whatever we were doing, she nailed it in one'.

It's fair to say that up until this performance, Amy had been happy to drift along on life's tide, both unsure and uncaring about where the current's ebbs and flows might take her. Suddenly, with a full orchestra behind her, everything made perfect sense. This, she knew, was where her destiny lay. And slowly but surely, people were beginning to take note.

As a backdrop to the events slowly shaping Amy's future, she'd started dating an aspiring singer-songwriter called Tyler James, whom she'd met whilst attending the Sylvia Young Theatre School. Tyler was no slouch in front of the microphone either, and within a couple of years, the Yorkshire-born singer would be hailed by *The Face* as being 'Britain's answer to Justin Timberlake'. The movers and shakers over at the *NME* were also championing him as 'one to watch', but though Tyler would sign to Island/Universal in 2003 and make the playlist at Radio Two, as well as making an appearance on *Top of the Pops*, his star wasn't destined to ascend any higher, and he was dropped from the label in 2005.

Though Amy might well have achieved recognition of her own volition, it was Tyler who provided the 'Divine Spark' which set an unstoppable chain reaction into motion. Tyler happened to be signed to Brilliant, a recently incorporated management company that was a sub-division of music mogul Simon Fuller's 19 Management. Brilliant was a two-man operation headed by Nick Godwyn, who before taking the reins had handled the PR for the Spice Girls at Fuller's behest. But when 'girl power' got a bit ahead of itself and the cocksure Spice Girls unceremoniously gave Fuller his P45, Nick felt honour-bound to tender his resignation. And it was in return for this show of solidarity that Fuller – who was no doubt already formulating ideas for what became the *Idol* franchise as a means of ensuring no girl or boy band would ever again gain the upper hand – generously offered to fund whatever ventures Nick fancied trying his hand at. Nick chose to follow Fuller into music management, which is how he came to be sitting in the main chair when Tyler, Brilliant's sole client at the time, slid a demo tape containing one of Amy's songs across the table. 'I really wouldn't know how difficult it is to get record company attention because I was never in a position

*Amy casually dressed in an Adidas jacket and tracksuit bottoms in March 2004, six months after the release of her debut album* Frank.

where I was shopping myself round going, hi, this is me and my product,' Amy told *M* magazine in June 2004. 'By the time I got a record deal, I already had publishing and management in place. I got my break through my friend Tyler who'd been working with these A&R guys. They were in a car one day and Nicky [Shymansky] said, "There's this girl on the radio singing jazz, we could use her," and me mate Tyler says, "Nah, I know someone who's a wicked jazz singer!" And that was it.'

The song in question was called 'Estrogenius'. Today, Nick Godwyn likens it more to a poem than a song, and though the badly-played guitar accompaniment left plenty to be desired, the voice was emotive enough to leave the hairs standing up on the back of his neck. Despite Tyler's repeated assurances, he simply couldn't believe that the voice on the tape belonged to a sixteen-year-old schoolgirl. He was, however, savvy enough to recognise that if this was what a low-grade tape-recording of her voice could do to his heartstrings, then the possibilities once he got her inside a professional studio were limitless. And with that in mind he asked Tyler to invite his girlfriend to come to the office for a chat.

She was 'young, fresh and curious, with huge eyes, and even bigger lashes', said Nick, remembering that first inauspicious meeting at his office in 1999. As she'd been told she'd be expected to sing something at the meeting Amy brought along her baby guitar, but whilst tuning the instrument she inadvertently snapped a string. And that, at least as far as Amy was concerned, was the end of the audition.

Everyone knows the age-old adage that one never gets a second chance to make a first impression. And in the music world second bites at the cherry are as rare as second comings. Nick himself freely admits that aspiring hopefuls crossing the office threshold had, at best, a one-in-ten chance of redeeming themselves. But there was something so utterly enchanting and disarming about Amy that he invited her to go away and think things over, and said she should give him a call if she fancied giving it another go.

♪ ♪ ♪

Amy did fancy giving it another go, and returned the following week to give it her all in her own inimitable fashion. Whether or not she did so with the baby guitar remains unclear. But then again, it was Amy's vocal chords rather than her fret skills that Nick, and his nineteen-year-old A&R (artist and repertoire) sidekick Nick Shymansky, were interested in. They instantly knew from the moment Amy cleared her throat that she was something special, immediately recognising that the giggly, doe-eyed innocent sitting cross-legged on the opposite side of the table was capable of making the whole world sit up and listen if she could deliver that same vocal every time. The only fly in the proverbial ointment – and it was a pretty big insect – was Amy's self-doubt. She wasn't sure if she even wanted to be a pop star.

This sounds incredible given that she'd spent her formative years enrolled at various performing arts-orientated schools, but while she was curious about the two

Nicks, and the music industry as a whole, Amy had never really stopped to consider that her gift might actually earn her a living.

Mitch Winehouse also had misgivings, but these had more to do with whether Brilliant was a reputable company than doubts over his daughter's talents. But the two Nicks assured Mitch that, though they couldn't possibly give solid-gold guarantees that Amy was destined for stardom, they promised him faithfully that they would look after his daughter every step of the way. And that, should the journey fail to be a profitable one, they'd do everything in their power to ensure it was a memorable one. 'Looking back, it seems ludicrous, but we really thought, if it [Amy's record] doesn't sell, who cares?' reflected Nick Godwyn. 'If she's having a good time, then we're all happy. We were idealists and naive, but I was loving it.'

Naivety aside, there was no doubting the two Nicks' enthusiasm for – and commitment to – the Winehouse cause. And with Mitch proudly standing by her shoulder, Amy scrawled her signature on the contractual dotted line.

> **'My friends used to go to lots of pop gigs but most of the people I loved and wanted to see play were dead. It kind of limited my options.' – Amy Winehouse**

Now that they had their girl, the next step was deciding what to do with her. It didn't take long for the two Nicks to realise Amy was no ordinary sixteen-year-old. Most girls her age were listening to the Top Forty countdown and following the requisite fashions, whereas Amy eschewed the drivel emanating from daytime radio and *Top of the Pops*. Her perennial hit parade featured Etta James, Billie Holiday, Ella Fitzgerald, Lena Horne, Dinah Washington, Carole King, James Taylor, and, of course, Frank Sinatra. But Amy didn't simply view these legendary artists as inspirational icons; she saw them as extended members of her family. If this wasn't atypical enough, Amy didn't just listen to their back catalogues either; she studied every groove of every album, absorbing the music until she was an authority on the genres – particularly jazz. While her girlfriends sat debating whether the Spice Girls could carry on without Ginger, Amy would be pondering how Sarah Vaughan seemed to sing around the notes of the song or how jazz pianist Thelonious Monk could make one instrument sound like a five-piece band. 'My friends used to go to lots of pop gigs but most of the people I loved and wanted to see play were dead,' Amy later lamented in an interview with the *Independent*'s Fiona Sturges. 'It kind of limited my options.'

Indeed, though her favourite TV show was Channel Four's long-running *Countdown*, Amy was so knowledgeable about forties and fifties jazz that she probably could have made a name for herself away from the microphone on BBC One's recently rejuvenated *Mastermind*.

Rather than rush Amy into a studio for an immediate cash-in, the two Nicks devised a cunning plan to keep their protégé under wraps and away from prying industry eyes while an expert team was assembled to work on Amy's material and image. That they succeeded in their task for the best part of three years suggests the two Nicks could have had a career in espionage. While keeping an act squirreled away for such an inordinate length of time may have gone against every music industry rule, we have to remember Amy was still only sixteen. And aside from learning her craft – the way she wanted to learn it – she was still maturing as a young woman. Thankfully, Amy was unconcerned with the money and fame aspects of what she was doing and remained one hundred percent focused on the job in hand throughout. But while keeping Amy under wraps didn't hit them too hard in the pocket, dedicating four years to developing an act was not without risk, for who was to say Amy wouldn't opt for an alternative career somewhere along the way?

Even more amazing, given that they themselves were starting out and had no other bankable acts on their roster, was that they waited three years before securing Amy a record deal. But there was method to their madness because, as Nick Godwyn sagely pointed out, the pressure mounts almost from the moment an artist signs a record deal. And that pressure will filter through to the artist, regardless of how good or seasoned the manager.

♪ ♪ ♪

The time-honoured tradition of garnering record-company interest in up-and-coming talent is by way of a promotional pack, which usually features a highly-polished demo tape featuring the best material on offer and a bio of the artist in question. Having worked with several record companies in the past, I know that the majority of such promo packs end up – unopened – in the A&R office bin. And Amy was astute enough to know that posting off a demo tape along with her hopes and dreams would be a waste of time and effort. 'I didn't go knocking on people's doors,' she told the *Belfast Telegraph* in February 2007. 'I wouldn't bother sending anybody your tape. [A&R] People get tapes by the sack-load, and a lot of the time they don't care.'

But with the two Nicks having patiently watched from the sidelines as Amy honed her talents, there was never any question of their wasting a stamp. They knew beyond question that what they were selling would bring buyers aplenty, and on discovering that the industry was abuzz following the leak of a couple of Amy's demos, they decided it was time to enter the arena.

With several big-hitters making appreciative noises about the leaked demos, the two Nicks scheduled a meeting with the MD of Virgin Records. But when the minute-hand struck the appointed hour, there was no sign of Amy. While an hour can seemingly flash past in the blink of an eye if you're out on the lash, or in the arms of a loved one, it's an interminably long time to make small talk with someone you've just met. They finally managed to locate their errant charge, and one can imagine the Virgin head-honcho's chagrin on being informed that Amy – a London girl born and bred – had got lost and given up the ghost, and didn't even think it necessary to make the call.

Fortunately, Mr Virgin was in a benevolent mood – either that, or he was desperate to get Amy on the label's roster – and the meeting was rescheduled for the following afternoon. This time Nick Godwyn wasn't taking any chances and dispatched his namesake to collect Amy. As the minutes ticked towards the meeting hour it must have seemed like déjà vu for Nick, only this time with his partner also missing in action. With the minutes ticking down to the reappointed hour, Nick and Amy burst through the door looking as though they'd both spent the morning scavenging on the local landfill site. It seemed Amy had suffered a panic attack at the thought of what she perceived to be signing her life away, and Nick had wrestled her into a skip and kept her there until the storm clouds blew over.

Though several companies including EMI – with whom Amy had signed a lucrative publishing deal several months previously – were making overtures and waving record contracts, Amy signed with Island Records. Nick Godwyn claimed that one of the reasons they settled on Island Records – which had been home to Mott the Hoople, U2, and Bob Marley during the initial stages of their respective careers – was because their offices and recording studio were housed within a north London townhouse not too far from Amy's home, so she could wander over without getting lost. But there is a far more romantic aspect to the tale; for once again fate's fickle fingers were to guide Amy's hand.

Not long after Amy had signed her publication deal with EMI, Darcus Beese, who was head of Island Record's in-house A&R team, was listening to a tape featuring a collection of songs from respected songwriting siblings Steve and Pete Lewinson. Beese was instantly captivated by the soulful vocal featured on several of the songs, but when he asked for the singer's name he was inexplicably informed that they'd only been allowed to procure the girl's services by swearing faithfully to keep her name a secret. Despite his repeated pleadings, the Lewinson brothers refused to divulge their secret, and it would take Beese months of painstaking detective work before he finally uncovered Amy's identity and made the necessary call to Nick Godwyn.

Getting the go-ahead from Island Universal's CEO Lucian Grainge was little more than a formality for Beese, however, as Grainge readily understood the precocity of Amy's talent. The deal was drawn up and duly signed at the offices of Brilliant's solicitors at midday on 22 December 2002, the last working day of the year before the Christmas break. Once again, Amy inadvertently managed to mess things up by turning up at the offices of EMI Publishing, where bemused staff must have wondered what was going on. But the champagne was simply allowed to chill a little while longer – because if something is worth having, then it is worth waiting for.

Though it had taken longer than Sylvia Young, or any of Amy's other teachers would have predicted, the girl from Southgate was finally on her way.

# 2. I Told You
# I Was Trouble

**'I don't ever want to do anything mediocre.
I hear the music in the charts and I don't mean
to be rude, but those people have no soul.'**

Amy might have signed a recording contract but that didn't mean she was suddenly going to turn over a new leaf, or even make much of an effort to fall into line. With pound and dollar signs wafting on the horizon, some managers might have tried to stamp their authority and bring their artist into line, but Nick Godwyn – who had suffered all the tantrums and torments Spice World could throw at him, and survived the ride without too many additional wrinkles – was more sympathetic than most towards Amy's absent-mindedness and her other foibles. He knew that her forgetfulness and recent tardiness were merely cogs in Amy's well-oiled defence mechanism. For unlike the vast majority of wannabes, who would have no doubt readily sold their soul along with their grandmother to sweeten the deal if it meant securing a record contract, Amy had dragged her feet to the contractual table. Her reticence, however, had nothing to do with her holding out in the hope of a better deal, but rather her uncertainty about committing; as though in signing the contract she'd somehow given away a part of herself that could never be redeemed. 'My management tell me off,' she told the *Guardian* in May 2004. 'Not tell me off but say, "Go and apologise to these heads of the record company." I'm like, "Okay, fuck it, cool, let's go. I'll apologise, I don't give a shit [. . .] Sorry, sorry, sorry, sorry. It's just a word, innit?'

One didn't need to be unusually perceptive to understand Amy. Sure, she could be difficult, and disruptive – but then again, what teenager isn't? Those born with a

*Strike a pose: A poised Amy proves she's comfortable in front of the camera
in 2004, long before the paparazzi became a regular fixture in her life.*

prodigious talent are perhaps attuned to a drum cadence that the rest of us mere mortals fail to hear. Nick Godwyn was bang on the money when he said that Amy's talents were beyond her years, and that she was constantly playing catch-up with her voice. Theatre aficionados will already know that torch songs such as 'As Long as He Needs Me' from *Oliver*, 'I Don't Know How to Love Him' from *Jesus Christ Superstar*, or 'I Know Him So Well' from *Chess* are performed by actresses who are – shall we say – of a certain age, as an ingénue couldn't possibly be expected to convey the lyrical potency to an audience. Yet had Amy so desired, she could have mastered any one of those numbers, and there wouldn't have been a dry eye in the house.

But to say Amy made the transition from backroom singer to global superstar overnight would be doing certain individuals something of a disservice. One of the key unsung heroes in polishing the proverbial diamond in the rough was a west-London producer known only by his nom de guerre, 'Major'. Nick Shymansky had formulated a plan to hook Amy up with a producer with a feel for an 'urban' sound, someone who would understand that Amy's jazzy vocal style would best suit a more contemporary context. Sometime in early September 2001, Nick inadvertently discovered that the guitar player Amy was currently working with on song ideas had a producer friend who went by the name of Major. A quick fact-finding mission would have revealed that Major was a talented DJ and MC who had worked with Soul II Soul. And his stock would have risen further when Nick heard about the *NME* lauding Major as having the ability to create a backing track unlike any other.

This was literally music to Nick Shymansky's ears, for he knew that bringing out the best in Amy required a producer who was willing to smash the barriers rather than be content to see how far they might bend. Having obtained Major's number, he made the call and arranged a meeting for the following Tuesday.

Of course, Tuesday, 11 September 2001 will forever be a date of infamy, owing to it being the day that nineteen al-Qaeda terrorists hijacked four United Airlines aeroplanes and declared war on America. With the world focused on the incomprehensible events unfolding before its eyes, as thick plumes of black smoke billowed out from the twin towers of the World Trade Centre and up into the sky above Manhattan, when Major arrived at Brilliant's offices he wasn't unduly surprised to find that no one was much interested in discussing music. But when Nick finally played Amy's demo tape, Major was stunned into silence for a second time that day.

Being an aficionado of hip-hop and R&B, Major unquestionably understood where Nick Shymansky was looking to go with Amy, and was happy for Nick to arrange a day for Amy to go to his home studio in Kensal Rise. As it happened, he'd recently dusted off his old Nina Simone albums, and had immediately recognised that Amy could be the 'noughties' answer to naughty Nina (who died from breast cancer whilst Amy was recording *Frank*). 'I didn't wanna influence Amy by playing her that stuff,' he said in *Amy Amy Amy*. 'But, in my mind, I had the route I wanted to go with her.' After establishing some common ground and breaking the ice by messing around with some of Nina's classics such as 'Strange Fruit', 'Born Under a Bad Sign', and 'My Baby Just Cares for Me', they got down to more serious work.

By the end of the session Major had several new demos in the can, which wasn't a bad afternoon's work by anyone's standards. But if Major was struck by Amy's ability to spontaneously come up with lyrics as though conjuring them from thin air, it wasn't until the second session – held again in Kensal Rise – that he truly came to understand the potency of her magic.

Amy had spent the weekend partying with friends in Southampton and was making her way back up to London by train when the Major called her to get a guestimate of her expected arrival time. He'd spent much of the weekend creating the backing tracks, and was so excited about one in particular that he played it down the phone. By the time Amy reached Kensal Rise she'd penned a lyric relating to her not-so-lost-weekend, and a half-hour or so later the finished song, 'Alcoholic Logic', was recorded, mixed, and in the can. 'She [Amy] basically wrote up her weekend, is what she did,' said Major. And while alcohol would have undoubtedly flowed in the forming of their friendship, it was 'Alcoholic Logic' that served to bond Amy and the Major professionally. 'I can express myself. I'm not an idiot. I'm not frightened of appearing vulnerable,' Amy told the *List* in February 2007. 'I write songs about stuff that I can't really get past personally – and then I write a song about it and I feel better.'

> **'I can express myself. I'm not an idiot. I'm not frightened of appearing vulnerable. I write songs about stuff that I can't really get past personally – and then I write a song about it and I feel better.'** – Amy Winehouse

Over the coming weeks the collaboration intensified as – with the Major's other projects permitting – the two would hole up in his basement studio to work on new song ideas. Had Amy's fretboard skills been up to scratch, it's fair to say that no one, other than perhaps Nick Shymansky, would have been allowed to infringe on their Kensal Rise domain. But eventually they conceded defeat and invited renowned session guitarist Ian Barter to sprinkle some of his six-string sparkle onto the proceedings. Indeed, according to Major, it was Barter who taught Amy how to really play the guitar. 'I just used these jazz chords that I was learning at the time, and that was it,' Amy told the *Big Issue* in July 2004. 'The first song I ever wrote [while studying for her GCSE music coursework], I did it in three minutes. And I was like, this is easy. And I could do better as well. That's when I realised that I wanted to write some serious music.'

The vast majority of the 'rare' and 'unreleased' demo recordings that can be found on bootleg CDs and DVDs at Camden Lock, and other markets around the world, can often seem rather monotone and lifeless coming through the speakers. Then again, they are only meant as a guideline for those involved in the recording process, and not for public consumption. But if the industry excitement surrounding Amy's leaked demos was anything to go by, then it's fair to say that the tracks created in Major's home studio would have been a bootlegger's dream.

Aside from helping Amy formulate her sound, Major also claims to have been instrumental in bringing her talents to the attention of Island Records through his friendship with Darcus Beese. According to Major, it was his playing one of the demos down the phone, rather than the tape of Amy's work on the Lewinson brothers' tape, that first set Beese's A&R antennae tingling. On hearing Amy's sultry tones, Beese pleaded with Major to set up a meeting with her as soon as his calendar allowed. Yet though island's A&R chief was desperate to meet Amy, he was equally anxious to keep at least one of his cards close to his chest. So while it was okay for Major to let Amy know who was coming to dinner, so to speak, he wasn't to reveal how his friend earned his corn.

The July 2007 edition of *Spin* magazine (which featured Amy on the cover) goes some way in confirming Major's story, as Beese is quoted as revealing that he snuck into Brilliant's offices to see if he might find out who was handling Amy. But given that the two Nicks were doing everything in their power to keep Amy's talents firmly under wraps until the time was right, it's highly unlikely that they wouldn't have spotted a furtive fox sniffing about the hen house.

All that really matters, of course, is that Beese got his girl, and the moment where Amy wows Lucian Grainge and Island/Universal's other high-flying execs is depicted in the accompanying documentary to the *I Told You I Was Trouble – Amy Winehouse Live in London* DVD (Universal 2007). Amy, dressed casually in shirt, jeans and boots, sings from the comfort of an armchair, backed by an acoustic guitar, while the boardroom suits look on agog.

On securing Amy's signature for Island, Beese told *HitQuarters*, the music industry publication regarded as an A&R man's Bible, that he felt the reason behind the excitement over an artist such as Amy, who was an atypical pop star for the time, was due to what he saw as 'a backlash against reality TV music shows, with audiences becoming starved'.

One thing that isn't in dispute during this frenetic period in Amy's life, however, is that she teamed up with songwriting duo Stefan Skarbek and Matt Rowe to begin writing songs which would hopefully make up a sizeable portion of the track-listing on her as-yet-untitled debut album. It was immaterial which label ended up first past the winning post, but it was vital that Nick Godwyn had Amy primed and cocked for when their corporate paymasters began calling the shots. Because with Brilliant being wholly reliant on Simon Fuller's benevolence, if Amy didn't start swimming upon hitting the water, there was every danger that Brilliant would sink along with her.

While the two Nicks entered the contractual-negotiations minefield with Island,

*All that jazz: Amy succumbs to a fit of laughter during her performance at London's Jazz Café in January 2004.*

Amy headed into Mayfair Studios in Primrose Hill with Stefan and Matt. 'I didn't think I was particularly special,' Amy said in a *Hospital Club* interview in 2006. 'All my friends can sing, so I was like, shhhhhh, whatever. You know how most kids get a degree and then they go and do music, so they've got something to fall back on? Well, music was my thing to fall back on. I thought, whatever happens, I can always go and do music. Then I thought, fuck it, I wanna career. It was weird 'cause it just fell in my lap. I was doing some gigs and then they offered me studio work. I was like, why are you offering me studio time, and he was like, 'cause you're gonna do an album eventually, and I was like, *what?* I was sixteen and I was like, what are you talking about? And I had a record deal by the time I was eighteen. It was mad.'

The trio soon struck up a relationship similar to the one Amy had developed with Major and Ian Barter, and though on occasion Nick Godwyn called upon the additional services of songwriter Felix Howard, it was usually just the three of them making up a Mayfair ménage à trois. Working in the intimate confines of the recording studio, it's fair to say that the three male songwriters may well have developed feelings for Amy that were above and beyond a professional nature – especially when you

> ## 'I had a record deal by the time I was eighteen. It was mad.'
> ### – Amy Winehouse

consider many of her songs were chock with sexual references and innuendos. And given Amy's open attitude to casual sex, and her assertion that 'cheating on people is fine; like smoking a spliff', who knows what may have occurred behind closed doors had she not been smitten with her first serious boyfriend? She'd met the boyfriend in question whilst working at WENN. His name was Chris, and he was a few years older than she was. And that, for the moment at least, was all she was willing to reveal.

When the *Guardian* tracked down the relevant parties following the success of *Frank*, Felix Howard recalled his first encounter with Amy. 'She showed up for our first session wearing a pair of jeans that had completely fallen apart with "I love Sinatra" embroidered on the arse. I just fell in love with her.'

The studio clock may have been slowly racking up the pennies, but Stefan, Matt and Amy thought nothing of afternoons being given over to walkabouts through Regent's Park, or knocking back White Russian cocktails (vodka, coffee liqueur, and cream) in the trendy, upmarket bars of Primrose Hill. This was when the picturesque enclave was the drinking domain of the so-called 'Primrose Hill Set'; the clique of British actors including Jude Law, Ewan McGregor, Sean Pertwee, and Johnny Lee Miller. Amy's future pal Kate Moss was also a member of this select set, and the two could well have been drinking in the same bars. But Amy was still virtually unknown, and had yet to reach a level where their social circles might overlap.

There were also regular forays into Camden, where Amy was becoming something of a face on the scene due to her frequent appearances at the Dublin Castle pub, the legendary venue from which Madness had exploded onto an unsuspecting music scene a couple of decades earlier. Knowing that the two Nicks dutifully came over to the studio at 6:00pm each Friday to see how the week had gone, the trio would have to scurry back and cobble something together before their arrival. Though Nick Godwyn would probably beg to differ, seeing as Brilliant was picking up the studio tab, the shopping trips weren't complete idle follies, as forays into Camden's varied and offbeat music haunts provided an eclectic collection of sounds that were taken back to the studio to be discussed and dissected – and, wherever possible, assimilated into what they were working on.

Whilst the boys were pouring over the bargain-bin grooves in the sound booth, Amy would be in the kitchen pouring the tea. By all accounts Amy made a great cup of char, but while Stefan and Matt weren't averse to a cuppa from time to time, Amy's 'twenty a day' Tetley fetish put them in grave danger of tannin poisoning. Of course, hearing stories of Amy slurping endless cups of tea in the studio seems strangely at odds with the public's perception of the hell-raising harlot of later years. But while tearing it up in the studio might make for good copy in the rock'n'roll archives, it achieves little in the way of creativity.

Having improved her fretboard dexterity with help from Ian Barter, Amy was now keen to try her hand at the array of instruments one tends to find lying about a recording studio. One instrument that particularly caught her eye was a trumpet, which, of course, has long been associated with jazz. On discovering that Stefan was something of a whiz on the trumpet, she immediately began pestering him to teach her the rudiments. As with everything else in Amy's life, she gave learning the trumpet her all, which didn't always please the studio's other residents. According to Stefan, one who particularly found Amy's trumpet noodlings less than agreeable was Madonna, who was there recording demos for her *American Life* album. On hearing what sounded like a scalded goose running amok in the corridors, Madge sent one of her underlings to put the poor creature out of its misery.

Stefan, who would go on to write songs for Mel C following the Spice Girls' break-up, believes it was this relaxed, carefree atmosphere in the studio that provided the spark of creativity for many of the songs. Going into a recording studio already knowing the tracks you're about to lay down can be intimidating enough, so going in there with a blank canvas and no set pattern as to which paints you're going to use – while the studio 'quid-o-meter' is rising faster than the temperature – would be doubly daunting to most musicians. But, of course, Amy was no ordinary artist.

♪ ♪ ♪

The light-hearted, White Russian-infused atmosphere within the studio made for equally playful music. The boys would bounce ideas around until hitting on a melody they were both happy with, and as long as Amy didn't hunch her shoulders in a by now telltale show of displeasure, they knew they could roll with the flow. Amy's songwriting style was very much 'of the moment', as frivolous song titles such as 'I'm a Monkey Not a Boy' suggest. 'I want to grow as a musician – and then I can come back to [straight] jazz,' Amy told the *Guardian* in 2004. 'I want to write songs about how I see the world. But I'm never happier than when I'm singing jazz, happier even than having sex. Sex ends eventually, music never does.'

When they weren't fishing for melodies, Stefan and Matt, occasionally with Felix if he happened to be around, would clown around providing twenties-style, flapper girl-esque dance routines and backing vocals. For their ad hoc act they took to calling themselves 'The Cheesy Peas', in mock-homage to the seemingly unpalatable vegetable-and-dairy combo first immortalised on *The Fast Show*, which has supposedly gone on to become the ultimate student meal. But Amy had seen something in the trio's high-jinx japes, and imagine Stefan's surprise when attending one of Amy's shows in Los Angeles – where he now resides – in 2007, and seeing a troupe of male dancers performing a similar (and infinitely more professional, it must be said) routine.

Other song titles which Stefan remembers from the sessions were 'Ease up on Me', and 'Do Me Good', which would later resurface as one of the back-up tracks on the 'Rehab' single in 2006. Another song Stefan remembers with clarity was 'Ambulance Man', which Amy seemingly wrote off-the-cuff as a means of expressing her feelings about her Nan, Cynthie, who had been rushed to hospital earlier in the day. As he sat there accompanying her on the piano, like Major before him, he couldn't help thinking that Amy was connecting with something unseen from a higher plain.

But whilst Stefan's recollections of working with Amy are wholly positive, they are somewhat less rosy when it comes to those responsible for her development: namely Nick Godwyn. He believes that Godwyn's habit of bringing in a different producer to work on each new batch of songs led to occasions when there were too many chefs overseeing the soufflés. Though she was still learning her craft, Stefan could sense that Amy had a pretty good idea of what musical direction she wanted to take, yet to his mind the two Nicks appeared intent on dragging her down a darker, more serious path. He feels that they were wrong to stifle her lighter side, if only because it was part of her personality. But singers singing inane ditties about monkeys do tend to have short shelf lives. It's also worth pointing out that, aside from her occasional performances with the National Youth Jazz Orchestra, Amy's stage experience to date consisted of playing the back rooms of pubs.

Of course, Stefan's observations regarding Brilliant's supposed failings may also stem from the fact that the two Nicks deemed the majority of their collective efforts unworthy of Amy's debut album. Though happy to have allowed the songwriting trio a fair degree of latitude in the studio – if only to get Amy's jazz-juice flowing – Brilliant's 'dynamic duo' were close to sealing the Island deal and couldn't allow anything or anyone to derail the gravy train now that they were so near the station.

Upon hearing *Frank*, however, Stefan would at least have the grace to recognise that – in his words – he and Matt Rowe simply didn't have the tools at their disposal to bring out the best of Amy. He wasn't referring to the facilities at Mayfair, because the studio had state-of-the-art equipment – as Madonna recording there readily testifies. No, the principle tool he's referring to is 'je ne sais quoi', that special something so indefinable that we have to borrow a colloquialism from the French.

Amy, though undoubtedly fond of her three 'Mayfair amigos', had come to realise a jocular jazz album – although fun to make, would be detrimental to her career prospects. 'Making the album I was very focused,' Amy told *Word* magazine in 2004. 'Maybe in years to come I will be a good collaborator but at that point I was, like, "Look, here is my music. We need brass on this, or that needs to be faster." And I don't want strings. If you want to work with me and you love strings, then go home.

'I probably earned a reputation as a difficult person, because I wrote my own songs and I didn't need people in the studio with me. Not to be rude, but these people would be trying to write pop songs! And I would say, "Who are you writing for? What session are you on? Get out." But then I'd waste a day trying to be nice to the person. I'd waste studio time letting them do what they wanted; because I thought it would be the polite thing to do.'

Had this been the 1970s, Brilliant's manifesto in regard to Amy's career would have been to get Amy her own prime-time television show à la Lulu, Cilla Black, and Nana Mouskouri. In the seventies Britain could still remember the days when jazz was a major force, both musically and culturally, and Amy – aside from plugging her own material – would have invited the likes of Cleo Laine, her hubby Johnny Dankworth, and Humphrey Lyttelton to belt out a few jazz standards. But this was 2002. If jazz was going to appeal to a 21st-century audience, then it would have to come with an entirely fresh approach. And this was why only two songs from those summer-long sessions would make it onto her debut album.

♪ ♪ ♪

With her sizeable share from the EMI and Island deals swelling her bank balance, aside from saying sayonara to Stefan and Matt, Amy also made her first tentative steps on the road of independence by moving into a flat in Camden Town with her old school pal, confidante, and fellow singer-songwriter, Juliette Ashby. 'I don't have many extravagances in my life,' Amy told the *Guardian* in 2004. 'So with my deal and that I was able to get myself a nice base. It's always gonna be mine.' As Amy threw clothes and toiletries into a bag, one could almost hear Janis Winehouse telling her daughter that 'cleanliness is next to godliness'. But as any student will tell you, Mr Sheen and hoover-bags come in a very poor second to beer and weed.

The two girls had first befriended each other back at Osidge Primary School in Southgate. One of Amy's abiding memories from infant school is of her and Juliette

pretending to be pop duo Pepsi and Shirlie, who, despite releasing two albums and several singles in their own right, will perhaps always be best known as Wham's backing band. And though both girls were always up for a bit of mischief, it seems Amy was already showing signs of her fearless nature that would come to the fore in later years. Whilst reminiscing about her famous former flatmate in 2007, Juliette told the *Observer* how one of them would suddenly get up from their desk and rush out of the classroom in a fit of tears. As the teacher couldn't possibly be expected to leave the class unattended, this would allow the other to offer to go and see what was troubling their friend. The two would then go off in search of an empty classroom to hide out in until the end of the lesson.

The Pepsi and Shirlie routine was only one of their whimsical musical collaborations. Another being when the two decided to form their own rap act along the lines of American female hip-hop trio Salt-N-Pepa. Having decided on the name 'Sweet 'N' Sour', with Amy taking the role of 'Sour', they took turns on Juliette's electric guitar writing suitably 'killa toons'.

Camden, of course, was already regarded as the epicentre of London's counterculture scene. But following the explosion of Britpop and the emergence of good ol' fashioned rock'n'roll guitar groups such as Oasis, Suede, Blur, Elastica and Echobelly, there really was no other place for an aspiring musician to be. Indeed, on any given night, Noel, Liam, Damon, Alex, Justine, et al – or the 'Camden Caners' as they came to be known – could be found tearing it up at the Good Mixer on Inverness Street.

When Amy wasn't attending meetings at Island HQ, or sounding out jazz musicians for the impending debut album, she lived life like any other young woman finding herself free of parental restraints for the first time. She was happy to work hard, but only as long as she could play harder. And if they weren't acquainting themselves with the colourful clientele of Camden's pubs, the two girls whiled away long evenings putting the world to rights over a spliff or three. For contrary to the public's jaundiced perception of Amy's subsequent lifestyle, though hard drugs would inevitably find their way onto the menu, at this time in her life weed was her only drug du jour. Indeed, to her mind people who relied on Class A stimuli to get through the day were just 'arseholes'.

As anyone who has smoked weed on a regular basis will know, imbibing 'da 'erb' allows you to free your mind without having to worry whether any other parts of your anatomy will follow. The only drawback to embarking on an ethereal journey is that more often than not you return to terra firma with a compelling urge to eat almost anything to hand. This is known to potheads everywhere as having the 'munchies'. And though chocolate and sugary sweets, such as the syrupy strawberry laces the girls had devoured at school, are best at quelling the rumblings, according to Juliette, Amy

*A fresh-faced Amy promotes* Frank *at an HMV in-store performance, January 2004.*

would think nothing of roasting a chicken at three in the morning. It seemed Amy just loved feeding people, and whenever the stress levels threatened to go into overdrive, she would retreat to the kitchen and begin preparing mountains of food.

♪ ♪ ♪

Unlike writing a novel, when the storyteller has upwards of 80,000 words with which to weave their intricate tale, a songwriter is usually expected to do the same in a couple of verses and a chorus. The most enduring compositions are, of course, ones that stir the emotions. Songs of love found, love lost, and love unrequited. Though Amy probably didn't see it at the time, it was Chris's decision to bring their relationship to an end that stirred her to pen the songs that would solve the problem of deciding exactly which musical direction she should take.

Every other contemporary musical genre has its torch songs, be it the blues, country, grunge, opera, pop, rock, or R&B. Hell, even punk has a few tearjerkers in its collective canon, so why not jazz?

'I would say that jazz is my own language,' Amy told the *Guardian* in February 2004. 'We [Amy and her friends] all love Missy Elliott, we all love Timbaland and Magoo, we all love Stevie Wonder, but no one shares my taste for the older stuff. From the age of eleven I was listening to Ella [Fitzgerald], who would sing the song perfectly but in a straight way, and then I learnt about subtlety. I heard people like Sarah Vaughan use her voice as an instrument, and that inspired me so much because it made me realise that a whisper can be so much more effective than just belting something out.'

While Amy was in that dark place that we all have to visit from time to time – going through personal hell, or cathartic cleansing, depending on one's outlook – Darcus Beese was busy whittling his way through a shortlist of producers he believed capable of harnessing Amy's sound and taking it to a new level; those who might add their own indelible sheen to the magic. For though Major would have been the automatic choice, he was unavailable as he was on the other side of the world touring with Soul II Soul.

During his occasional visits to Mayfair Studios, Beese couldn't help but notice that whenever Amy was away from the microphone she'd be listening to the American rapper Nas, whose last two albums, *Stillmatic* (2001) and *God's Son* (2002), had been co-produced by Salaam Remi. Perhaps more important – at least in terms of Island recouping its not inconsiderable outlay – was that the Miami-based producer, going under the moniker 'The Chameleon', had also lent his expertise to the English R&B singer and rapper Ms Dynamite's Mercury Prize-winning, platinum-selling crossover debut album *A Little Deeper*, which, of course, featured the UK Top Five hit 'Dy-Na-Mi-Tee'.

'As a musician, I need to have music to play my children when I'm older,' Amy told the *Independent* in April 2004. 'I'm going to want to play them the music that I was listening to when I was twenty and what is there? Nothing. It's dry. I'll be playing my children Ms Dynamite every day.'

Remi – thirty-one when the offer from Beese to produce Amy's debut album came through to him at his Creative Space Studio – was the son of musician and studio engineer Van Gibbs. Though he'd set off on his musical adventure intent on being a drummer, and had been given his first set of drums at the age of three, his first taste of life in a recording studio – largely due to his dad producing the record – came when he played keyboards on Kurtis Blow's 1986 album *Kingdom Blow*.

His father's being old school meant that Remi, as he now preferred to be known, had easy access to a wide variety of instruments, and over the years he became proficient on drums, piano, keyboards, and the guitar. But it was his fascination with hip-hop and sampling that led to him first thinking about becoming a producer. He'd tutored himself by painstakingly analysing the recording and production techniques on his father's old James Brown records, and when it came time to build his own studio he set about sourcing vintage equipment that would have been considered state-of-the-art when the Godfather of Soul was getting up and doing his 'thaang'. This not only proved time-consuming, but also very expensive. However, his layout and dedication were both duly rewarded when, in 1996, he was invited to work with the Fugees on their album *The Score*, which became a multi-platinum bestseller.

> **'From the age of eleven I was listening to Ella Fitzgerald, who would sing the song perfectly but in a straight way, and then I learnt about subtlety.'** – Amy Winehouse

Though a native New Yorker, the 9/11 attacks on the city had left Remi feeling uneasy, and he moved his studio kit and caboodle down to Florida, where he expanded his already impressive portfolio by working with the likes of Toni Braxton, Wyclef Jean, Lisa 'Left-Eye' Lopes, and Mis-Teeq.

Bizarrely – or so it must have appeared at the time, given that multiple producers overseeing Amy's sessions with Stefan Skarbek and Matt Rowe at Mayfair Studios had proven counter-productive – Island elected to split production duties on the album between Remi and Commissioner Gordon (aka Gordon Williams), who'd already made a name for himself working with the likes of KRS-One, Will Smith, and Whitney Houston, before firmly putting himself on the map by working on former-Fugee Lauryn Hill's 1998 debut album *The Miseducation Of Lauryn Hill*, which entered the *Billboard* 200 chart at number one.

By assigning not one but two renowned producers to the debut album, it was obvious that Island wouldn't be pulling any punches from here on in. But while most newly-signed artists would surely have suffered a seizure at the thought of going into the studio with such heavyweights, Amy simply shrugged her shoulders and got on with setting her recent heartache to music.

# 3. To Be
#     Perfectly Frank

'I'm a musician. I'm not someone who's trying to be diplomatic, you know, trying to get my fifteen minutes. I'm just a musician who is honest.'

In October 2003, Island Records finally tested the Winehouse water by releasing 'Stronger Than Me' as the lead single from Amy's forthcoming debut album, *Frank*.

Looking back now, it's astonishing to think that the release date of the track that would win the Ivor Novello Award for 'Best Contemporary Song' the following year doesn't get so much as a mention in the *NME*'s 'Top Fifty Singles of 2003'. There's no mention of the parent album in the magazine's 'Top Fifty Albums' of the year, either. It appears that the only release deemed newsworthy for Monday 20 October – the day the triple-platinum-selling *Frank* went on sale in the UK – was Britney Spears's supposed comeback single 'Me Against the Music', featuring Madonna, with whom she'd famously got up close and personal onstage at the MTV Video Awards a couple of months earlier. Whilst it might not have been everybody's idea of televisual entertainment, feigning French kissing her pals Madonna and Christina Aguilera in front of a worldwide audience when she had a new album in the pipeline – not that the troubled Britney needed any more exposure – would have had her label bosses and management team reaching for the champagne.

Yet despite Island's hard sell garnering a clutch of enthusiastic reviews, 'Stronger Than Me' would stall at very disappointing number 71 on the UK singles chart – the lowest chart placing of Amy's career.

One can only wonder what the label's promotion and marketing teams would have given for photos of a scantily-clad Amy snogging a global megastar to be plastered across the front pages of every newspaper in the land.

*Old soul: Amy during a promotional trip to Rotterdam in March 2004.*
*'I'm so proud of it, you know,' she said of* Frank, *her first album.*

♪♪♪

As any self-respecting A&R guy will tell you, when breaking a new act you have more chance of success with a band than with an unknown solo artist. A band will have already been bloodied in front of a live and often hostile audience, be writing its own songs, and have an image that can be marketed. Irrespective of Amy's talent, to have any hope of establishing her in what was a highly-competitive market she was going to need either a killer image, or a killer debut single; something along the lines of Dusty Springfield's 1963 debut 'I Only Want to Be with You', Britney Spears's 1999 debut '. . . Baby One More Time', or even Lady Gaga's more recent 'Just Dance'. A song with a melody so infectious that it would – in Nick Godwyn's words – have a milkman in Newcastle whistling it on his rounds. Yet for some unfathomable reason, given that Island's outlay thus far was only matched by the label's expectations, the mournful 'Stronger Than Me' was chosen as the debut single. And what makes *Frank*'s subsequent success even more amazing, given the fickle nature of Britain's record-buying public, is that it's the opening track on the album.

> **'I'm not here to be famous, I just want to challenge myself. If it all goes wrong, I'll have my music.'** – Amy Winehouse

The packaging also left much to be desired. Because while we've all come to know the tattooed and beehived Amy, parading about in all her rat-combed, biker-moll glory, her metamorphosis into a latter-day Ronnie Spector was still some years away. Photographs from the period show a curvaceous young woman more than capable of striking a sultry pose; yet the cover shot chosen for Amy's all-important debut single, with her wearing a nondescript pink top and a garish Hawaiian-style skirt, looks as though the photographer has come into the room and caught the babysitter unawares.

The song itself would also catch people off guard, for instead of a rabble-rousing, jazz horn-blaring intro to get people jumping out of their seats and onto the dancefloor à la her later, hugely successful cover of the Zutons' 'Valerie', a lilting guitar and bass riff silkily shuffles out of the speakers almost unnoticed. It's only when the syncopated beat eventually kicks in, suffused with teasing whiffs of alto sax and sixties pump organ, over which accomplished jazz guitarist Binky Griptite adds his flighty licks, that the listener realises that although what they are hearing is traditional old-style jazz, it's also very much of the here and now. In essence, this was Amy's reward for all those hours spent pouring over her dad and nan's record collections. Because it gave her the prudence to know that in order to take something forward, you have to know where it's been. 'I've always loved jazz,' Amy told *M* magazine in June 2004. 'My brother introduced me to Thelonious Monk by saying, "If you like Miles Davis, you will love Monk." He was right. Monk woke me up to the fact that jazz was much more than mood music. As for getting into someone like Roy Ayers, it was Salaam who said, "You gotta listen to Roy." My mum loved Carole King's *Tapestry*, that was always in the house. But man, there are so many wicked contemporary people I love, I mean, Missy Elliot, obviously. She is a powerhouse. Then there's Mos Def – love him.'

When reviewing *Frank*, the BBC's Greg Boraman would cite 'Stronger Than Me' as having all of the qualities to prove 'that jazz-influenced contemporary soul needn't be safe or sullied by the dinner or "smooth" prefixes'. After praising Amy's debut for being made with 'such assurance, confidence, and to such instant acclaim', he rightly opined that many far more seasoned artists would readily trade in their gold discs for Amy's distinctive 'twenty a day voice'.

As we now know, the lyric to 'Stronger Than Me' is a femme-power blues anthem narrating Amy's disgruntlement at her erstwhile lover Chris. She always saw *Frank* as a concept album, not so much *Songs for Swingin' Lovers!* as songs for stinging an ex-lover, who being seven years older, should, to her mind at least, have been the one taking control of every aspect of their relationship; the most important being in the bedroom. She even goes so far as to accuse her 'lady boy' of being gay, which would have been bad enough had it been a private attack on his perceived lack of machismo. But of course, with Amy's star steadily rising, the muck-raking media would have gone all out in unearthing his identity. 'I don't hate men or anything,' she told the *Guardian* in response to questions about her boyfriend-baiting lyrics. 'But the things I said about him in that song were through frustration because I liked him so much and I knew that he liked me. But just because you have a connection with someone doesn't mean that it's going to be smooth running. Life isn't like that.'

But as accomplished as the tune undoubtedly is, it is Amy's soulful delivery that really grabs the attention. One could be forgiven for thinking the voice they are hearing is that of a seasoned New Orleans chanteuse whose heart has been breached more times than the city's decaying levees, not that of a nineteen-year-old Jewish kid from north London. 'I'm not here to be famous,' she told the *Evening Standard* in 2004. 'I just want to challenge myself. If it all goes wrong, I'll have my music.'

♪ ♪ ♪

Released onto a largely unsuspecting public, *Frank* entered the UK album chart at number 60. The album's title supposedly alludes to the candour and honesty of Amy's lyrics, while of course another explanation could be that it was named in homage to her idol Frank Sinatra. But it's also worth remembering that at the time Tony Blair's Labour government had launched its £3 million 'Talk to Frank' anti-drugs campaign, which was aimed at alerting both parents and teenagers to the dangers of 'street' drugs such as cannabis, cocaine, and ecstasy.

Someone should have had a frank discussion with those at Island HQ who were responsible for the album's artwork, as once again they failed to make more of a play on Amy's musical leanings. For while having a black and white shot of Amy standing in front of a vintage Electro-Voice stand-alone microphone and done up to look like Billie Holiday in her heyday would have been clichéd, the Charles Moriarty shot of her walking what appear to be two dogs pulling her in either direction (given that she's holding two leads) through a deserted Soho at night, in an off-the-shoulder pink number, was hardly going to get the message across. The image not only jars with the album's lyrical content, but looks comical when juxtaposed with the 'Parental Advisory Explicit Content' sticker. Indeed, the only hint we have that Amy isn't your average 'girl next door' is one of the accompanying photos – snapped by Valerie Phillips – of her poised with a spliff in her hand. And though we're constantly told never to judge a book – or in this case an album – by its cover, that's exactly what we do.

Those who did purchase a copy during those slow-burning first few weeks of sales would have soon realised that 'Stronger Than Me' wasn't the only song that Amy had drawn from the dark and murky depths of her own turbulent soul. Her uncanny aptitude for documenting the events unfolding within her world would become her trademark. Yet though the heartache over her split with Chris would provide plenty of introspective inspiration, no subject was considered sacrosanct; not drugs, not casual sex, not even her parents' divorce. 'Being personal is my style,' she told the *Independent* in 2004. 'That's me. I'm never going to say things that other people have said in the same way. It wouldn't be interesting for me to hear it so it's not interesting for me to say it.'

In hindsight, Island's bosses might well have chosen the more uplifting (no pun intended) and up-tempo 'You Send Me Flying' to open the album. With its strident drum beat and disco piano, over which Binky Griptite plays some of the most exquisitely crisp jazz guitar ever committed to vinyl, the sharp-nailed ballad narrates what again feels like an autobiographical tale of love gone wrong. Amy's voice on this track is reminiscent of disco divas Donna Summer and Diana Ross, juxtaposed with more sedate stirrings akin to Sarah Vaughan and Sade in their soul-stirring prime. Or perhaps Island's intention all along was to lull the listener into a false sense of familiarity before unleashing Amy's more modern urban jazz sound.

'I wrote those songs [on *Frank*] so that people would love them and be able to hear them and say, that's me, like I do when I listen to music,' Amy told *City Life* magazine in November 2004. 'That's what I really hope for. It sounds so poofy, but that is what it is, really. And when they do that, it's a really beautiful thing. I love *Frank*, I'm so proud of it you know, but it was a big old fucking melting pot, there's so much on it, which makes for a wicked live show but . . . I don't know, maybe if I do an album that pretty much all sounds the same, the set will be really boring.'

'Know You Now', a skilful fusion of vintage R&B and classic seventies Motown soul, with a sunny Caribbean twist thrown into the mix, sees Commissioner Gordon taking over from Remi at the mixing console. 'I feel grateful to him [Chris] for a lot of

*Stronger than me: Amy looks defiant onstage at her Shepherd's Bush Empire show in May 2004.*

stuff. Because, basically, I'd never been with a man I had any emotional connection with before,' she told the *Daily Telegraph* in 2004. 'I'd been with just big, stupid men. And I'd never have known there's nice, clever men out there . . . But those songs I wrote – that was hurt. Now, I wouldn't let myself get hurt like that.'

The resplendent 'Fuck Me Pumps' sees Amy castigating those, shall we say, less morally-inclined females who shamelessly gyrate about the dancefloor clad in their designer-tag next-to-nothings. 'Some women think they're validated by a wedding ring, or having a rich boyfriend. But they're not things you should strive for. So it's about those kinds of girls,' she told *Times Online* when asked about the song. 'But there's so many bitches out there, I can't take it . . . No, I'm all for girls being together. But I'm a bitch, what can I say? [. . .] No, I'm not a bitch. Not all the time.'

Next up is the short, but deliciously sensuous 'I Heard Love Is Blind', one of those laidback 'love gone wrong' songs that conjure up images of Billie Holiday or Lena Horne standing onstage in a smoke-filled basement room, baring her soul to the microphone. 'Moody's Mood for Love', the standard jazz classic first popularised by King Pleasure half a century earlier, has a sultry calypso flavour owing to Earl 'Chinna' Smith's reggae licks dancing in and out of Remi's busy bass. And once again Amy delivers a vocal which is seemingly beyond her years. 'That's a whole other phase of my career,' Amy told the *Guardian* in 2004. 'Round sixty, when I can't grasp reality any more, that's when I'll go to Las Vegas and sing standards and, trust me, I'll kill 'em.'

'There Is No Greater Love', an even older jazz standard by Isham Jones and Marty Symes, is all midnight-mood piano and understated bass, again evoking images of Billy, Dinah, and Sarah. 'As an artist the key things you have to do is prove yourself in a live scene,' Amy would later say when asked about the inclusion of the two covers on the album. 'To prove yourself in a writing scene, and prove yourself doing covers. They're as important as each other.'

With the cover versions – or reference points – out of the way, we are invited back into Amy's modern-day world with the salaciously-titled 'In My Bed'. 'The song actually came about after I'd had sex with an ex-boyfriend,' she told Pete Lewis for *Blues and Soul*. 'I was like "Now get out of my bed and take a cab home!" Then, when he said he had no money, I gave him a tenner and told him goodbye! While I have written about times in my life that have given me trouble and there are points on the album where I am really upset and really angry, I'll always put a punch-line in there and I'll always make it funny.'

It doesn't take a genius to figure out the identity of the ex in question, but a closer inspection of the scathing lyric reveals just how far Amy was thinking outside the box. During the mixing of the album, Amy, Mitch Winehouse and Nick Godwyn were sitting around the table in Nick's office listening to a demo of the song when Mitch casually enquired as to the meaning behind the somewhat ambiguous couplet: *'The only time I hold your hand / Is to get the angle right.'* Without batting either of her mascara-laden eyelids, Amy said that it was about a guy masturbating her. But while 'girl power' has undoubtedly empowered females everywhere to feel confident in their sexuality, and talk openly with each other about what they might do in private, how many girls would dare to discuss something so personal with their dad?

'Take the Box', which is undoubtedly the album's standout ode to love's lost dream, is also the closest we get to a pop song in the traditional sense. The lyric, which is more of a commentary on a break-up, resonates with women everywhere. It's not only about the man being handed his possessions in the time-honoured fashion as seen in countless films, it's also about the woman compartmentalising her memories of better times. As Amy told the *Sunday Herald*, 'When my first boyfriend split up with me, it was something I really couldn't make sense of. I didn't understand why, so I wrote "Take the Box" about how I literally had to put all his [Chris's] stuff in a box and get rid of it. That's a good example of how that sorted me out.' It was also another example of her uncanny aptitude for documenting events unfolding within

> 'When my first boyfriend split up with me, it was something I really couldn't make sense of. I didn't understand why, so I wrote "Take the Box" about how I literally had to put all his stuff in a box and get rid of it.' – Amy Winehouse

her world, which would of course soon become her stock in trade. 'I don't ever want to do anything mediocre,' she subsequently told the *Independent* in February 2004. 'Learning from music is like eating a meal. You have to pace yourself. You can't take everything from it all at once. I want to be different, definitely. I'm not a one-trick pony. I'm at least a five-trick pony.'

To the uninitiated, 'October Song' (one of the two Skarbek/Rowe songs to make it onto the album), with its lilting Caribbean soul grove, conjures up images of someone in their autumn years reflecting on past events in their life. In fact, it is Amy's lament for her dead canary. And this – on a subliminal level at least – is evident in the lifting of the melody from 'Lullaby of Birdland', the 1952 jazz standard recorded by Ella Fitzgerald and Sarah Vaughan amongst others. According to Stefan Skarbek, Amy had gone away for the weekend, forgetting to feed the canary in question, and was near-disconsolate on returning to find it lying, claws upturned, at the bottom of its cage.

'What Is It About Men' sees black rock getting it on with soft white rock, yet has the unmistakable groove of Lauryn Hill, while the highly infectious 'Help Yourself' – which serves as something of an open letter to an older lover (Chris?), telling him to either sort out his act or clear out his closet – is another laidback, horn-led fusion of reggae rhythms, acoustic guitars and lumbering bass. There were others, however, who thought their own actions had provided the song's subject matter. 'My dad said, "You've got to stop talking about me, you're making me sound like a serial philanderer!"' she told *Totally Jewish*. 'I never actually said that though. The song "What Is It About Men" is about infidelity, but I am very close to both my dad and my mum. I'm a lot like my dad. We're both the sort of characters who believe it's important to get stuff done and to be honest with people.'

*Frank*'s closing track is the other Skarbek/Rowe co-composition, 'Amy Amy Amy', a woozy jazz number that gallops along as though straight out of a Chicago speakeasy rather than a Camden Town enclave. If Stefan Skarbek is to be believed, the song was penned in mock-homage to Amy's then current, but unnamed boyfriend, which would have to be Chris, given that he was the only known boyfriend Amy had during this period. Stefan says they took to calling the boyfriend 'Mr Mushy Peas' on account of his turning up at the studio to escort her home each evening carrying a tray of chips and mushy peas from a nearby fast-food outlet. The song materialised following Stefan's on-the-spot response of, 'Oh, Amy, Amy, Amy', when she told him that she'd ended the relationship.

The album plays out with 'Amy Amy Amy (Outro)', a slice of improvised jazz over which the MC signs off in a manner befitting an intimate live performance rather than a studio recording. In days gone by, the stylus crackling as it rode out the song's final groove would have listeners walking across to the gramophone, but they'd be only halfway there when the outro suddenly drifts into a lilting soul/jazz refrain. A few heartbeats later it fades out, to be replaced by a classic soul-inspired beat, with Amy calling softly to us over horns and crisp guitar. And then, as if indeed by magic, the album unofficially plays out to the hidden track 'Mr Magic', all soaring horns, and then finally silence. 'The thing that always drove me with *Frank* was human interaction and that will always drive me,' Amy told the *Word* in early 2004. 'Relationships and how fucked up they can get. I guess that'll always inspire me.'

♪♪♪

It was perhaps inevitable, with the British music industry's movers and shakers preoccupied with what they were calling the 'new jazz' scene, that Amy would be lumped in with Jamie Cullum, Nora Jones, and Katie Melua. Of course, such pigeonholing has long been something of a parlour game pastime for the world's music press. After all, the Beatles had been thrown in with Gerry and the Pacemakers and Billy J. Kramer and the Dakotas as part of the so-called 'Merseybeat Explosion'; the Sex Pistols, the Clash, and the Damned were punk's 'unholy trinity', Spandau Ballet, Duran Duran, and Visage were all hopeless new romantics, while Nirvana, Soundgarden, and Pearl Jam – along with every other Seattle band of the time – were amalgamated as 'grunge'.

But in order for a nascent scene to thrive, it requires a spiritual home: somewhere where like-minded groups can perform, and where fans can genuflect before the altar. The Beatles and the other Merseybeaters had the Cavern, punk had the 100 Club (which ironically is a time-honoured jazz club), the new romantics had the Blitz Club, while grunge had the Off Ramp Cafe. But while the early pioneers of London's fifties jazz scene – those 'Absolute Beginners' Colin MacInnes immortalised in his 1959 novel of the same name – had a plethora of smoke-filled clubs in and around Notting Hill to lay down their groove, when Amy, Jamie, Nora, and Katie were first starting out, they had to sing for their respective suppers wherever they could find an empty stool.

And in hindsight, whether 'new jazz', or 'pop jazz', was even a scene remains very much to be seen. To the best of my knowledge, of her three supposed fellow 'new jazz jivers', Amy only ever appeared on the same stage as Jamie, so where, other than in the myopic media's blinkered eyes, was this supposed scene? If anything, it's likely it was merely a marketing ploy aimed at shifting a few more units.

When she was starting out Amy was probably grateful that the music press wrote about her – or if not grateful, then at least sensible enough to know when to keep quiet. But now that she had an album shortlisted for a couple of Brit Awards ('Best Female Solo Artist', alongside Sophie Ellis-Bextor, Jamelia, Annie Lennox, and eventual winner Dido; and in the 'Best British Urban Act' alongside Mis-Teeq, Dizzee Rascal, Big Brovaz, and eventual winner Lemar), there was no need to keep her caustic tongue clamped between her teeth. The wheel was still spinning, but now she had plenty of chips to play with. 'People put us together because we have come out at the same time, but we're nothing alike,' she seethed during an interview with London-based online music publication *Music OMH* in early January 2004, by which time *Frank* was riding high in the charts and selling like . . . well, like hot cakes. 'I feel bad for Jamie being lumped in with me and her [Katie Melua]. I'm a songwriter and she [Melua] has her songs written for her. He must feel frustrated. She must think it's her fucking lucky day.' But Amy wasn't finished, not finished by half. 'If anyone stands out straight from us, it would be her. It's not like she's singing old songs like Jamie, she's singing shit new songs that her manager [renowned songwriter Mike Batt, the man who also gave us the Wombles] writes for her.'

When the aforementioned punk band the Clash first started out, their manager Bernie Rhodes suggested that they should write songs about what was happening to them; what was happening in their world. And whilst she was holed up in her own Camden hideaway, Amy obviously tore a page or two from Bernie's Clash manifesto when penning the songs that found their way onto the album. 'Being a musician and a singer, there is always going to be something in me that is completely twisted, fucked up and sad,' she would subsequently tell the *Times* in 2003, shortly after the album's release. 'But I don't want to be stuck in a room where all I ever do is write, lie there and cry, and then write a song.' But she would also define her songwriting as being therapeutic, allowing her to indulge her dark side and work through her personal problems: 'I only write about stuff that's happened in me . . . stuff I can't get past personally. Luckily, I'm quite self-destructive.'

Though touring and performing in front of an audience is a necessary part of any professional singer's itinerary, Amy was undoubtedly happiest in the recording studio.

'Yeah, to play and sing live for me is like just going on auto-pilot,' she told *Blues and Soul*. 'I'm not there to be like, "Hi everyone! If you don't have my album, go and get it!" It really is just a case of me wanting to please the crowd by giving the songs their just due every night, mainly because I'm really, really proud of them.'

Going into the recording studio for Amy must have been akin to entering a synagogue, in that she was leaving the outside world and all its unnecessary distractions at the door. She was working with musicians who were all looking to achieve the same goal – to make the best record possible. But while said musicians only need to focus on making sure their fingers are where they're supposed to be on their respective instruments, Amy would need to detach herself from her surroundings and enter that secret, spiritual place deep inside herself, where her genius ebbed and flowed in time to her heart's syncopated beat.

> **'Some things on this album make me go to a place that's fucking bitter. I've never heard the album from start to finish. I don't have it in my house.' – Amy Winehouse**

With the exception of the two covers, the rest of the songs were either written solely by Amy, or co-written with Remi. 'Salaam drew me out of myself musically, because, while I'm a really wacky songwriter, he's exactly the same. He'll always strive for something really different. And I'd never met anyone who can tap into an artist the way he can; which to me is the mark of a great producer,' she told *Blues and Soul*. 'With Salaam I feel like musically anything can be done – and I've never felt like that when working in England, where they don't wanna listen to a girl who thinks she knows what she's talking about. Basically all they care about in this country is listening to the record company.'

But while Remi, Commissioner Gordon, and Binky Griptite, Earl 'Chinna' Smith, Teo Avery, Troy Genius, and the other musicians brought in to work on the album could all be proud of their contributions, a volcano was about to erupt over at Island's north London offices. For Amy was somewhat less enthused with the finished album, as the label had gone behind her back and included tracks and mixes that she believed were substandard. In an interview with the *Observer* shortly after the album's release, Amy let Island's bigwigs – and Nick Godwyn, who was equally culpable in her eyes – have both barrels. 'Some things on this album make me go to a place that's fucking bitter. I've never heard the album from start to finish. I don't have it in my house.' But the venting of her invective-brimming spleen didn't end there, and she proceeded to embark on a searing soliloquy lambasting the efforts of Island's in-house marketing and promotion teams. 'It's frustrating, because you work with so many idiots – but

*Amy at a promotional appearance in Birmingham in 2004. 'You couldn't ever tell Amy what to do,' said Nick Godwyn, her first manager. 'She did what she wanted. And we encouraged that.'*

they're nice idiots' – she added, softening her tone only slightly – 'so you can't be like, "You're an idiot." They know that they're idiots. I hate them fuckers, man. I've not seen anyone from the record company since the album came out and I know why . . . 'cause they're scared of me.' After pausing to draw breath and reload her sawn-off, she continued with her acerbic rant against Island's perceived failings. 'They know I have no respect for them whatsoever. Look, I know it's a terrible thing for someone to come out and say they hate their own music. It's the worst thing you can do. My album isn't shit. If I heard someone else singing like me I would buy it in a heartbeat.'

Amy's sassy, 'no quarter' approach to her music didn't only cause consternation in the recording studio and at Island HQ. She gave equally short shrift to anyone attempting to turn her into a 'media darling'. Some would say that promoting a new album – especially a debut album – is almost as important as the recording process itself. But instead of pouting and preening for the camera, Amy purposely went out of her way to alienate the media. Having already committed what those same 'some' would consider a cardinal sin by blithely ignoring an alarm call for an all-important Radio One telephone interview on her fellow 'lager ladette' Sara Cox's breakfast show, she proceeded to shock the show's 6.6 million early-morning listeners by turning the air blue.

She didn't even bother softening her edges when asked about her musical contemporaries. On being told that Dido – whose own 1999 debut album, *No Angel*, had sold in excess of 21 million copies worldwide – had been very complementary about *Frank*, Amy's caustic riposte was that she would rather pour cleaning fluid in her ears than listen to Dido. '[I mean] it's very flattering to be acknowledged, especially to be put with the women as opposed to the new artists,' she told the *Daily Telegraph* in January 2004, on being nominated for the 'Best British Female Singer' award at the forthcoming Brits ceremony. 'I feel like I've jumped a step. But it's Dido's award, really, isn't it? She has to get it so everyone can kind of justify why they bought her album.'

Pop's perennial princess, Kylie Minogue, was a 'one-trick pony', while Madonna, who had recently been declared the 'best-selling female rock artist of the 20th century' by the Recording Industry Association of America, was summarily dismissed as being 'an old lady'. 'She [Madonna] should get a nice band, just stand in front of them and sing.'

The media naturally seized upon what they saw as a desultory slur against the one-time queen of pop, and decried Amy as being rude and arrogant. But had they stopped to consider Amy's remark in its proper context, they would have seen they were confusing arrogance with confidence. For if they'd thought to question Amy further they would have discovered that she'd grown up listening to Madonna, and had near worn out the groove on her copy of *The Immaculate Collection* album. Following the advent of punk, haven't we come to expect pop's latest heir-apparent to belittle those that have gone before? At the time Amy had only recently turned twenty, whilst Madge was in her mid-forties and only a couple of years younger than Amy's own mother.

♪ ♪ ♪

'I pride myself on being different from everyone else, not on being the best singer or songwriter,' she told *Totally Jewish* in 2005. 'I am influenced by so many people – Ella Fitzgerald, Dinah Washington, Minnie Riperton and lots of others.' Of course, comparisons of Amy's voice with Billie Holiday, Dinah Washington, and Sarah Vaughan et al had been doing the rounds long before she even went into the recording studio to work on the album. And so when writing up the album for their respective editors, those reviewers seeking more contemporary similarities cited jazz and soul divas such as Mary J. Blige, Macy Gray, and Sade, while the *Guardian*'s Beccy Lindon described Amy's voice as 'somewhere between Nina Simone and Erykah Badu . . . at once innocent and sleazy', while the *Daily Telegraph* said, 'North Londoner Winehouse is nineteen, writes like Cole Porter, sings like Billie Holiday, plays snooker like a pro.' Over at the *Times*, however, Dan Cairns resisted making any outright comparisons – past or present – and instead opined that 'Winehouse has channelled an adolescence immersed in jazz, soul and hip-hop into a beguiling hybrid that, in the debts it owes, drops all the right musical names of yesteryear, but simultaneously manages to sound thrillingly new'. He ended by declaring *Frank* to be a 'staggeringly assured, sit-up-and-listen debut', that was 'commercial and eclectic, accessible and uncompromising'.

> **'I'm probably already a diva, if that means that you don't give a fuck about opinions. All I know is that I don't suffer fools gladly. I'm not here to make friends.' – Amy Winehouse**

When it was finally released in the US in November 2007, *Frank* shifted a respectable 22,000 copies in its first week, and the reviews were equally enthusiastic. *Billboard* magazine proclaimed *Frank* to be 'stellar', while lauding Amy's vocal as 'wobblier than now, yet still astounding'. Nate Chinen at the *New York Times* also took time out to praise Amy's original lyrics, and described the album's musical style as a 'glossy admixture of breezy funk, dub and jazz-inflected soul'.

In light of what eventually came to pass, US critic Douglas Wolk's 2010 retrospective review of *Frank* for *Pitchfork Media* would prove eerily prophetic. Aside from expressing a mixed response towards the album's themes, and connecting them to Amy's public image at the time of its release, Wolk wrote, 'in the light of her subsequent career, *Frank* comes off as the first chapter in the romantic myth of the poet who feels too deeply and ends up killing herself for her audience's entertainment'.

As for the lady herself, she subsequently said, 'I'm probably already a diva, if that means that you don't give a fuck about opinions. All I know is that I don't suffer fools gladly. I'm not here to make friends. I've learnt that the hard way – I used not to say things like "I really want to hold a guitar in my video", because I was trying to make everyone like me. But I don't give a shit now. At the end of the day I'm there to do my job. I'm not there to have picnics.'

# 4. Ready or Not, Hear I Come

'I'm not religious at all. I think faith is something that gives you strength. I believe in fate and I believe that things happen for a reason but I don't think that there's a high power, necessarily. I believe in karma very much though.'

While Remi and Commissioner Gordon were mixing their parts of the album in their hometown studios in Miami and New Jersey respectively, back in London Nick Godwyn took tentative steps towards Amy taking *Frank* out on the road. His first port of call was Paul Franklin at Helter Skelter booking agency. He in turn made the call to his former booking manager turned music promoter Christian Barnes, the driving force behind the recently-established 4 Sticks Live. Having listened to the demo Franklin had sent him, and liked what he heard, Barnes booked Amy for a trio of dates at the Cobden, an upmarket private members' club on Kensal Road in West London, the first of which was scheduled for Tuesday, 22 July.

At first glance, it seems strange – given that Amy was signed to Island Records and had an album in the process of being mixed – that Nick Godwyn would view Amy playing somewhere like the Cobden as a strategic career move. But it's worth remembering that, up until this juncture, Amy's biggest shows to date had been those at the Dublin Castle and various other pubs on the live circuit the previous year. While Amy's first performance at the Cobden was little more than a glorified open-mic night, the club's sedate setting was perfectly suited to bolster her confidence for the journey that lay ahead. When Amy next appeared at the Cobden on Monday, 11 August, on what was again billed as an 'emerging acts' night, she did so with a full band.

Given Amy's subsequent success and exposure, it is perhaps to be expected that Christian Barnes would remember booking Amy to appear at the Cobden. But with 4 Sticks Live having booked hundreds of nights like these, he could be forgiven

*Pretty in pink: Amy at the Prince's Trust Urban Music Festival, held at London's Earl's Court in May 2004.*

for failing to remember her performances. 'We've seen thousands of artists at the Cobden over the last four years. To remember an individual performer they must be very special. Amy was in that category. She didn't have the hits like "Rehab" back then, but she always had the voice.'

When Amy returned to the Cobden for her third and final show on Monday, 1 September, she did so with only a keyboard player as accompaniment. Though only five weeks had passed since Amy's first appearance there, and the album was still several weeks away from release, there was a real buzz around town by now and the 300-capacity club could have sold the tickets three times over. Though Paul Franklin had neglected to mention that Amy was signed to Island when he'd sent the demo across, Barnes sensed that big things were going to happen for the diminutive girl who stood five-feet two-inches in her stocking feet. Indeed, it wasn't long after Amy's final appearance at the club that he began seeing billboard posters advertising *Frank* on the Underground whilst making his way to and from home. Of course, another reason for Barnes remembering Amy's final appearance at the Cobden could be that, by pure coincidence, Annie Lennox happened to be in the audience. At the time, Annie

> **'I've got a sharp tongue, but there's humour in there as well. Also, I may be knocking my boyfriend, but I knock myself as well.'** – Amy Winehouse

was putting the finishing touches to her third solo album, *Bare*, in a nearby recording studio, and had only popped into the Cobden to sound it out as a possible venue for her impending solo tour. She wouldn't have known Amy had she tripped over her in the street, but by the time she'd finished her opening number Annie was a fan. 'I was completely blown away,' she told the *Times* in 2007. 'She [Amy] was like a woman in her thirties, with a whole seasoned delivery, not fazed by anything at all. I was in awe of her. I thought "wow", you have a special talent. God, you are eighteen, where did that come from?' Amy was in fact just two weeks or so shy of her twentieth birthday, but was still considered a raw talent compared to a seasoned pro like Annie.

The Winehouse clan were already proud of their Amy, but London's Jewish community was let in on the secret when the *Jewish Chronicle* – or '*The JC*', as it's affectionately known to its subscribers – ran an all-singing, all-dancing story on her achievements thus far in its 31 October 2003 edition. The London-based newspaper, which is the oldest continuously published Jewish newspaper in the world, had of course reviewed *Frank* on its release, a piece in which it challenged another – unnamed – publication for labelling Amy a 'feisty loose-tongued Jewish teenager from Camden', when her smoky vocal style had more in keeping with a 'feisty Jewish teenager from the Bronx, steeped in the Sarah Vaughan back-catalogue'. Though it made the usual comparisons with the jazz and soul divas of old, it recognised the dangers of giving the album a late-night jazz tag, and was equally wary of making comparisons between Amy and contemporary singers such as Sade, Macy Gray, and Mary J. Blige. That the *Jewish Chronicle* would think to feature an article on Amy, a local Jewish girl made good, is understandable, but seeing a risqué song title like 'Fuck Me Pumps' besmirching their periodical would surely have had its more orthodox readers reaching for the Talmud.

In its Halloween edition, the journalist introduced Amy to its readers who were as yet unfamiliar with her: 'If you saw her in synagogue, you'd think Amy Winehouse was your average north London Jewish girl, especially since she was brought up in a close-knit, middle-class family . . . but you'd be wrong.' Amy herself had been interviewed this time round, and on being asked to describe her music responded by saying her sound was 'very jazz based, with hip-hop and R&B influence, I sound like one of those old jazz singers'. And when asked to describe the inspiration for the songs on the debut album she readily admitted the majority were predominantly about her relationships with the opposite sex. 'I've got a sharp tongue, but there's humour in there as well. Also, I may be knocking my boyfriend, but I knock myself as well.'

♪♪♪

When one thinks of jazz, one tends to conjure images of Billie Holiday, Ella Fitzgerald, or Lena Horne standing at the microphone in a dark, smoky room reminiscent of prohibition-era Chicago. Between the final Cobden show on 1 September and the album's release seven weeks later, Amy played a handful of solo shows in similar surroundings, and also went out on the road as support to Jamie Cullum, whose third studio album *Twentysomething* was due out the same day as *Frank*. Of course, the Jamie/Amy billing only served to fuel the 'new jazz' flame. But the only new jazz on offer was that coming from Amy, because with the exception of a couple of tracks, the remainder of Cullum's album were either cover-versions or standards, whereas on *Frank* the opposite was true.

What many people didn't know about Amy was that behind the mascara-mask she was a shy, home-oriented girl, who looked upon what she was doing as a bit of fun before she – like any self-respecting Jewish girl – found herself a husband and had a family. Though she was now signed to a reputable record label, and had a debut album set for imminent release, she'd penned the songs on said album sitting alone in her bedroom, strumming the relevant open chords on her baby acoustic guitar. When writing their own material, most performers in search of mainstream success would dream of playing at Wembley Stadium, but it is unlikely that Amy thought beyond playing within close, intimate settings.

The release of the album, however, saw the bar raised in accordance with Island's expectations, and on Thursday 13 November, Amy made her 'large stage' debut at the Shepherd's Bush Empire. She did so opening for the Scottish-born reggae/jazz singer Finley Quaye, who'd started out in much the same vein as Amy a decade or so earlier before achieving mainstream success in 1997. It can take an artist years to learn how to handle a large stage – indeed, some never quite manage it. And though Amy effortlessly captivated the crowd with low-key numbers such as 'Stronger Than Me', 'I Heard Love Is Blind', and 'October Song', when it came time to raise the tempo her voice tended to sound harsh in the yawning three-tiered hall.

Now that Amy had bridged the gap between clubs and halls, Nick Godwyn decided it was time to up the ante even further by having her make the leap from support act to showcase headline. Just three weeks after her outing at the Shepherd's Bush Empire Amy returned to west London to play the Bush Hall on 2 December.

As she had done for her second outing at the Cobden back in August, Amy took to the hall's stage with a full band including a three-piece brass section, while she herself flitted between acoustic and electric guitar. Though *Frank* still wasn't making much progress in the UK album charts, thanks to the hype surrounding Island's latest acquisition, journalists from both the tabloids and the rather more austere broadsheets made the journey to the gig with pundits from the traditional music papers, to see if Amy's studio promise would live up to expectations on a live stage. The *Guardian*'s Caroline Sullivan, though critical of the choice of venue – as seeing Amy jostling for elbow room on the hall's compact stage somewhat spoiled the occasion – was enthusiastic in her praise for Amy herself: 'Her smoky, jazzy voice, subject of much acclaim, wrapped itself possessively around every bitter little lyric. And my, they are bitter. Winehouse is the very definition of potential. She's got some way to go before she matches Erykah Badu, to whom she's frequently compared, for emotion and technique [as she was by your newspaper, Caroline], but long may her angst unfurl.'

♪♪♪

After spending the Christmas break relaxing with her family, taking her dog Frank out for wintry walks, or creating havoc in Camden with Juliette, Amy got back to business and headed over to Island's townhouse HQ to discuss the strategy for forthcoming follow-up single 'Take the Box', backed with 'Round Midnight', which was scheduled for release on 12 January. Now that Amy was headlining her own shows, and meriting the attention of the broadsheet big boys, expectations for the single were high. Yet, for all Darcus Beese's talk about how well Amy was doing, having been short-listed for a couple of Brits, it was patently clear that the label wasn't wholly sure how best to market her – if only from the generic cover shot of Amy selected for the single, which wouldn't have looked out of place in an El Al Airlines advert. And though it would fare slightly better than 'Stronger Than Me' (a live version of which also featured on the single) by reaching number 57 on the UK chart, it didn't augur for a happy 2004.

*Best of British: Amy looking glam at the 2004 Brit Awards. 'I'm not the kind of person that would ever have gone if I wasn't nominated,' she said.*

Though Amy had long been 'unfurling the angst' – alluded to by the *Guardian*'s Caroline Sullivan – over constantly being associated with the 'new jazz' scene, it seemed she was growing equally incensed at having to defend herself against accusations that she was merely Simon Fuller's latest pop puppet. Given that Fuller had provided Nick Godwyn with the necessary funding to launch Brilliant, it was perhaps to be expected that those within the media with a grudge against Fuller – if only for inflicting S Club 7 and the even more ludicrous S Club 8 upon the world – would come after Amy all guns blazing. It's a wonder that Amy even bothered dignifying such claims with a response, as anyone who reads the tabloid showbiz columns knows that pop svengalis such as Simon Fuller and his namesake, Simon Cowell, are solely interested in making as much money as possible from their respective artists within a limited time-frame, before moving onto the next pretty face off the conveyer belt. Amy was serious about her music from day one, and would rather have taken a stall selling second-hand chewing gum on Camden Market than sell out to someone like Simon Fuller. Should any doubt have remained as to where she'd planted her flag in that regard, when being interviewed by the *Independent* in the days leading up to the Brit Awards ceremony, she launched a stinging tirade against the pop svengali's *Idol* franchise. 'I wouldn't have gone on one of those shows in a million, billion years, because I think that musicality is not something other people should judge you on. Music's a thing you have with yourself.' She took advantage of being in the media's glare to take a shot at Island's mishandling of her career to date, by railing against the music industry's ever-rolling publicity machine. 'I made my album and then they did what they wanted to it. They don't talk to me like I'm a person, they talk to me like I'm a product. If they've got a problem with me or the way my music sounds, I couldn't care less. They couldn't say anything to me that I haven't said to myself. I'm my own biggest critic. I've given them a lot of control. I made the music because I know how to do that, but then for the promotional side I stepped back and thought, "I've got to trust this lot," because I've never done this before. That was the wrongest [sic] thing I could have done. All they know how to do is what's already been done, and I don't want to do anything that's already been done.'

Though Amy came away from the Brits empty-handed, with plans underway for Amy's first headline solo tour, Island were keen to capitalise on the publicity that her nomination for two awards had generated in recent weeks, and on Monday 5 April, the double A-sided 'In My Bed'/'You Send Me Flying' was released as the third single from *Frank*. From a marketing perspective it would seem that Darcus Beese or someone else within Island's A&R office had caught Amy's recent rant in the *Independent*, as the cover shot used for the single was finally worthy of the songs on the disc, making a visual connection with the lead song's subject matter for the first time. Set against a shadowy city-scene backdrop, Amy sits in contemplative mood, looking for all the world as though she is indeed lamenting who she's allowed into her bed. Yet despite a massive promotional campaign – including extensive air-play – the single failed to find its target audience, i.e. the 6.18 million viewers that had tuned in to watch the Brits on television. And as Amy's fans had already purchased the parent album, and didn't therefore think the inclusion of the acoustic number 'Best Friend' merited the recommended retail price, the single stalled at number 60 on the UK chart, three places lower than 'Take the Box'.

If Amy was disheartened by the latest single's poor showing, which must have seemed like a backward step, you wouldn't have known it from her upbeat comments that same month in the *Independent*, which was now giving Amy so much column space that the paper was fast becoming her broadsheet biographer. 'I think that as my output increases people will realise that I'm in a class of my own,' she enthused. 'I'm different. I don't pride myself as being a great singer. I pride myself on being unique and on writing music that I would like to hear. That is what drives me.'

**'Musicality is not something other people should judge you on. Music's a thing you have with yourself.' – Amy Winehouse**

Amy's rapidly developing 'me-against-the-world' mentality where her career was concerned was also spurring her on at this time. Though Nick Godwyn undoubtedly wanted what was best for Amy, he was tainted through his ties with Simon Fuller. And while she was extremely close to her family (especially her dad Mitch, who was so vocal in his support that he'd gone so far as to take over from his daughter onstage during the second show of her two-night stint at the Pizza Express Jazz Club in Soho on 5 and 6 March, belting out a couple of Frank Sinatra classics), they could only really offer support and advice rather than professional guidance. For the two Pizza Express shows Amy had elected to perform with the Brad Webb Trio rather than her usual full band accompaniment. Mitch was so relaxed that he even took time out to berate Sam Beste, the trio's piano player, for what he termed 'doodling about' instead of just playing the tune straight.

But of course, Amy's buoyant mood could have simply been down to the news that all the venues on the forthcoming eleven-date tour – on which her old boyfriend Tyler James was to play support – had now sold out. 'I love being on tour, but I wish I could work off the crowd better; be more of a showman,' she would tell *Totally Jewish* in May 2005. 'For me, it's all about the songs, and I'm so busy concentrating on that, I'm not paying as much attention to the audience. I honestly never thought I would make any money from music. I figured I'd get a job in an office or as a waitress. I never had a great plan or promoted myself, but in a way I've been working for this for years.'

♪ ♪ ♪

The tour was set to get underway north of the border on 21 April, at Glasgow's Cottier Theatre, a former church situated in the city's trendy West End. That morning, the *Independent* – in what again could only be viewed as a flag-waving exercise given that the tour had sold out well in advance – carried an extensive interview with the tour's star under the banner headline, 'Amy Winehouse: Diva with a Stroppy Streak'. But judging from the opening paragraph, in which the 'new voice of jazz' is described as acting like a petulant schoolgirl who has just been given detention, it seems that Amy isn't too thrilled at having to repeat herself at this stage – even to the seemingly sycophantic *Independent*. 'Sorry, but it doesn't come naturally, talking about myself,' she said, purposely stifling a yawn. 'I don't see what's important about it. No offence to you, but I could be at my Nan's house right now. Or I could be waiting at home for the plumber to come and fix the washing machine.'

After eulogising about the album and how Amy might only be 'fresh out of her teens but carries the brash sentiments in her songs that suggest a woman twice her age and experience', the journalist tentatively enquires if Amy is perhaps being too hard on men? 'Not at all,' Amy fires back. 'I'm harder on myself than anyone else. Yeah, I've got high standards when it comes to me but it's important for me that the man I'm with feels like a king when I'm with him. And I want him to be the best he can be when he's with me. You know what? I reckon men are uncomfortable with anything that requires them to think. It's like when your mum phones you up and asks if you've paid your tax bill. You just block your ears and talk about something else.'

Taking the hint, the journalist steers the conversation onto Amy's early teens, and how she – like every other schoolgirl – had listened to staple pop icons of the day such as Kylie and Madonna, before finding herself drawn to the music in her parents' record collection. 'I liked the same music as all my friends, but I had my own ideas about what I could really listen to and what meant the most to me.'

And while she was once again content to discuss the media's seemingly never-ending determination to create a new pop jazz scene by pigeonholing her with Jamie and Norah, the mere mention of Katie Melua's name got her hackles rising. 'How ever much I know that she's shit, there are people that think Katie Melua is a real musician. That really gets to me.'

Unfortunately for Amy, the *Independent* didn't think to send anyone along to review her Scottish debut. And if the *Scotsman*'s less-than-complimentary review is anything to go by then – even if allowing for Amy suffering a severe bout of first night nerves – it wasn't much of a night to remember. The reporter charged with reviewing the show for Scotland's national newspaper was obviously a fan of both Amy and her music, and had gone along to the Cottier Theatre with every intention of eulogising Amy's performance: 'Of all the kittenish soul and jazz-loving youngsters who have made a play for the pop charts in the last few months, Amy Winehouse is the one with the

*Agent provocateur: Amy's outfit leaves little to the imagination onstage at the V Festival in Chelmsford, August 2004.*

most impressive voice. Her debut album *Frank* purported to be just that, revealing a forthright sexuality to rival that of Kate Bush's debut, *The Kick Inside*.'

Heady praise, indeed. But for those of Amy's Glaswegian fans who hadn't been able to get a ticket, from there on in the review made for painful reading. 'Unfortunately, during this gig the majority of her songs were coated in a standard issue jazz-funk veneer, which was tedious after five minutes, let alone an hour and five minutes.' Worse was to follow, as the *Scotsman* not only attacked her 'over-singing' vocal style, but dismissed her as being like any other 'competent *Pop Idol* wannabe'.

Thankfully however, the *Sun*'s review from the following night's show at Newcastle's Northumbria University proved infinitely more positive. 'Her music is a fusion of jazz, soul, funk, R&B and hip-hop styles, and you get the feeling that she reveals a little bit of herself with each of her songs. Her voice belies her age and her husky north London accent is transformed into a sultry jazzy drawl. Listening to her is like a sensual experience for the ears.'

> **'The Ivor Novellos are a songwriter's award and that's what I am. I'm not trying to be best female; I'm just trying to write songs.'**
> **– Amy Winehouse**

The next river city on the tour itinerary was Liverpool, for a show at the city's O2 Academy. After opening its review of the show with a desultory back-handed compliment about Amy looking like the lovechild of actress Penelope Cruz and Manchester United's Ruud van Nistelrooy, the *Liverpool Echo* went on to redeem itself by saying that seeing Amy live was an uplifting experience. But unkind comments about her resembling Man United's Dutch striker paled into insignificance when compared to the *Manchester Evening News*' scathing rebuke of Amy's performance at the city's Academy 2. 'Winehouse has been eulogised by the press and public alike, and one would expect a show to justify the hype. But she was found desperately wanting when it came to deliver the goods last Saturday night. She may have one of the most distinctive voices around, but talent does not a good show, nor an artist for that matter, make.'

Though she had little trouble holding her own in the recording studio, Amy was still finding her stride on the live stage, and as a result her skin had yet to thicken against such stinging criticism. It's fair to say that, had the day following publication of this review not already been designated a rest day, she might well have pulled a sickie. But Amy was nothing if not resolute and quickly shook off her Manchester mauling. However, according to contactmusic.com, the vibe was far more upbeat when Amy took to the stage at the Leeds Cockpit three nights later. 'In what seems like the blink of an eye this young Camden girl has become one of the most anticipated new British talents. Amy's down-to-earth approach and refreshingly honest lyric-writing bring the cool of the jazz greats into the 21st century with a relevance that is rarely seen.' The

*Observer* was equally appreciative of Amy's performance at the Norwich Waterfront the following evening and opined that if those gathered within the 'soulless Norwich venue' had closed their eyes, they would have been transported to a smoky jazz club in New York's Upper Harlem.

Perhaps not surprisingly, *Gay Brighton*'s fashionistas appeared more interested in what the devilish diva was wearing for her show at the Concorde 2 two nights later: 'Clad in figure-hugging vibrant red Adidas dress, with legs out, talons for claws, and a bold lightning bolt of a tattoo just below the palm of her hand, it's obvious that despite her soft, raspy voice, this is not a woman to be messed with.'

Following the tour's penultimate show at the Warwick Arts Centre on 2 May, Amy brought the curtain down on her debut headline tour at the Shepherd's Bush Empire. And this time, having exercised her lungs up and down the country over the past fortnight, there would be no criticism of her high notes – or any other note she sang that night. 'Shepherd's Bush is a perfect sized venue for me,' she later said. 'It's big but it's not Wembley, you know what I mean?'

And after taking a short but much-needed break to recharge her batteries, Amy appeared at the Prince's Trust Urban Music Festival, staged at the Earl's Court Arena over the weekend of 8/9 May, where she put in another smooth performance on a bill that included Beyoncé, Dizzee Rascal, the Streets, Jay Z, Mos Def, and Alicia Keys.

♪ ♪ ♪

On Thursday, 27 May, the 49th annual Ivor Novello Awards ceremony was held at the Grosvenor House Hotel on Park Lane. Though Amy had been nominated for 'Stronger Than Me', the general consensus within her camp – and indeed in everyone else's – was that the award would go to Kylie for her single 'Slow', which had hit the number 1 spot on both sides of the Atlantic. Or failing that, then Dizzee Rascal for 'Jus' A Rascal', from his *Boy in da Corner* album. But unlike at the Brits earlier in the year, it was to be Amy who walked up the carpet onto the stage to collect the prize. This was especially pleasing because, as Amy told *Music OMH* shortly after the nomination was announced, 'The Ivor Novellos are a songwriter's award and that's what I am. I'm not trying to be best female; I'm just trying to write songs.' And though the event wasn't televised, her victory at the awards would prove to be the snowball that finally triggered the avalanche, and within a matter of days *Frank* had shifted 200,000 copies, catapulting it up to number 13 on the UK chart.

Nick Godwyn, however, remembers this night as being the first time he became aware of Amy's polar mood swings. 'Nick [Shymansky] and I knew [that she'd won] before but didn't tell her so she got grumpy about that. We went back to the office and there were some flowers from the record company. She picked them up, scowled, and threw them in the bin. She'd already turned the day into a negative. Why would someone give her flowers? That was her. Dark and light.'

Amy remained unfazed by the reported surge in her album sales. Earlier in the year she'd told the *Guardian* that money wasn't as important to her as music and that she'd much rather live in a hole in the ground if it meant she could meet Ray Charles. 'I want to make the record company happy, and my parents worry,' she told the same paper. 'My Nan judges everything by the charts.'

Further award nominations came, as she was short-listed for the 2004 Mercury Music Award for *Frank*, and for 'Best Jazz Act' and 'UK Act of the Year' at the 2004 Mobo (Music of Black Origin) Awards – both ceremonies were scheduled to take place in September. Though undoubtedly thrilled at being nominated for the Mercury Music Prize, it was no doubt the two Mobo nominations which gave Amy – inspired and influenced by so many black artists – the biggest thrill.

> **'You know, I just sing and write reflecting everything I've ever heard. And, while there are white artists that figure in that, the people I listen to are predominantly black.' – Amy Winehouse**

'If someone actually did come up to me and say, "Hey whitey, get off my music!" Though I don't think that would happen! I'd be like, "I don't really understand where you're coming from,"' she told *Blues and Soul* in April 2004. 'I wrote my songs on a guitar; I went to a producer, and he did them for me. What's the problem? You know, I just sing and write reflecting everything I've ever heard. And, while there are white artists that figure in that, the people I listen to are predominantly black. But at the same time I'm never consciously like, "I'm gonna do that little Dinah lick there," or, "I'm gonna do that little Minnie Ripperton twiddle there." Because the minute I even start to think about what I'm doing I just lose it. I have to just shut my eyes and flow!'

Amy then made her Glastonbury debut, appearing on the legendary three-day festival's Jazz World stage at the end of June. This was followed by appearances at the T in the Park festival in Glasgow over the weekend of 10/11 July and the Summer Sundae Weekender in Leicester on 15 August; Amy then brought her summer outdoor frolics to a climax by appearing at the V Festival a week later. 'We had lovely moments and lots of laughs,' Nick Godwyn said in an article he wrote for the *Times*. 'I'll always remember the two of us, driving away from the V Festival, singing "Respect" by Aretha Franklin.' Thanks to the up swell generated by the Ivor Novello award, *Frank* had gone platinum, and it was while they were backstage at V that Nick presented Amy with a platinum disc before she went on. But once again Amy's mood swings were in evidence. 'I thought she'd be happy and backstage I gave her a platinum disc – she just shrugged angrily.'

*Amy at the 2005 Brit Awards, shortly before she began writing and recording* Back to Black, *the album that was to make her a superstar.*

On the back of *Frank* finally achieving platinum status, coupled with Amy having undertaken a solo UK tour and played all the major summer festivals, Island elected to release a fourth single from the album. As with 'In My Bed'/'You Send Me Flying', the label again opted to release a double A-side: 'Fuck Me Pumps' – truncated to 'Pumps' on the sleeve – coupled with 'Help Yourself' and backed with a live version of 'There Is No Greater Love'. As with the previous single, the packaging was worthy of its contents, and featured a striking cover shot of Amy looking every inch an FM diva. A clean radio edit – 'Pumps' – was recorded for commercial purposes in the hope that it would finally give Amy that as yet elusive Top Forty hit. But alas, this was not to be, as again Amy's fans didn't feel a live version of one of the album tracks merited the outlay, and the single stalled at number 65 on the UK chart.

♪ ♪ ♪

Though Amy was one of the nominees invited to perform at the Mercury Music Prize awards ceremony during the first week of September, her success at the Ivor Novello Awards wasn't to be repeated. Later that same month she was to walk away from the MOBO Awards empty-handed. But Amy was far from downhearted, as

> **'I love Marilyn Monroe. I wasn't born of these times. I should have been born in the forties.' – Amy Winehouse**

being nominated was evidence enough that her music was being appreciated where it mattered, and awards would only have to be dusted anyway. With the awards ceremonies out of the way Amy got on with rehearsing for her forthcoming second headline UK tour, which was set to commence at the Liquid Room in Newcastle on 4 November.

The twelve-date tour, which saw Amy return to Northumbria University, as well Manchester and Liverpool's Academies, also took her to Sheffield (Octagon), Nottingham (Rock City), Birmingham (Carling Academy), Folkestone (Leas Cliff Hall), and Southampton (Guildhall), and culminated in a sell-out show at London's 5,000-capacity Brixton Academy on 19 November.

The tour also saw her return to Norwich for a show at the city's University of East Anglia on the 10 November, and it was here that the *Norwich Evening News* caught up with her. 'Music is the only thing that will give and give and give and not take,' Amy said, adding that she didn't develop as a person until she discovered sex and sexuality.

The conversation then moved onto Amy's love of old films and her favourite sepia-toned screen idols of yesteryear – especially Marilyn Monroe. 'I love Marilyn. I wasn't born of these times. I should have been born in the forties.' It was only when the interviewer mentioned Cynthie Winehouse's criticism of Amy's public denouncement of her musical contemporaries – questioning why such a nice girl as her granddaughter would sound so rude – that Amy became animated. 'My nan does do that,' she snapped. 'I keep opening my mouth about people and we fall out because of it. We sit there and eat dinner and row. But' – she added in the same breath – 'she loves me. She doesn't care what I do. She is so lovely.' And to prove the point, she revealed she always carries a framed photo of Cynthie on her travels.

When asked for her thoughts on what an amazing year 2004 had been for her, Amy responded, "What happened to me last year, end to end, you think "Jesus Christ". I had an amazing year last year. I would never have imagined that Mos Def would become my friend, or that I would appear on *Never Mind the Buzzcocks*.'

As a means of winding down the interview she was asked to describe a typical Amy Winehouse gig. 'It's a bit raw at the gigs,' she said earnestly. 'I'm the kind of person who likes to get into it in a gig. I end up dancing. Plus' – she added, matter-of-factly – 'I don't like wearing many clothes onstage. I like to strut around. My look is not about trying to be sexy; it's about trying not to be sweaty.'

♪♪♪

With her touring commitments for 2004 at an end, Amy could afford to kick off her heels and look back on the year with some satisfaction. She had usually wowed the crowds wherever she went, and silenced those critics who'd said her voice couldn't carry beyond a club setting. *Frank* may have failed to break into the Top Ten after thirteen months of trying, and didn't have a Top Forty single to its name, but Lucian Grainge and everyone else at Island were happy enough with the album, while Nick Godwyn anticipated that a little extra promotional push over the impending Christmas high-street rush should nudge UK sales over the 250,000 mark.

The only downside to having a moderately successful debut album, of course, was that everyone at Island would now be pushing for better results with the follow-up. Darcus Beese and his team had nearly exhausted the marketing possibilities of the debut album, and the label bosses were making noises about Amy using the Christmas break to get down to some serious songwriting. In other words, just because she didn't have a boyfriend, while they were kicking back under the mistletoe with their respective better halves, she was expected to sit at home alone cooking up catchy choruses. But of course, therein lay the problem. The songs that made up *Frank* had been outpourings that resulted from the break-up of a serious relationship, and in order to be inspired she feared she would need to suffer similar emotional discord. 'I've taken pains to ensure I write of my time and that I write representing myself and people who are like me,' she told the *Daily Telegraph* in 2004. 'It sounds such a wank thing to say but I need to get some headaches goin' to write about.'

The only question was: with no significant other in her life, where were these figurative headaches going to come from?

# 5. I Can't Hide the Tears

'I had never felt the way I feel about him [Blake] about anyone in my life. It was very cathartic, because I felt terrible about the way we treated each other. I thought we'd never see each other again. I wanted to die.'

Though Amy would have sampled the delights of each and every one of Camden's watering holes upon moving to the area, it would be in the Hawley Arms on Castlehaven Road, just off Camden High Street, that she would choose to pull up a bar stool and call it home. And while the Georgian-fronted pub's ambiance and choice of alcoholic beverages would have been of huge importance, it's fair to say that its jukebox would have also come into the equation. Because aside from the usual fare of rock, punk, indie, Motown, soul and blues standards one would expect to find in any of Camden's other pubs, the Hawley Arms' juke carried a fine selection of pop nuggets from late-fifties and early-sixties all-girl groups such as the Angels, the Shirelles, the Dixie Cups, the Shangri-Las, and of course, the Ronettes. With her trademark beehive already taking shape, these two-minute bubblegum vignettes would – again, on a subliminal level at least – act as a sounding board for the musical direction Amy would take for her all-important second album. 'I like old sixties heartbreak songs,' she later told the *Times*. 'Girl-group comfort music; songs that you can sing into a bottle of whisky.'

It was whilst she was keying in her particular favourites one cold wintry evening in February 2005 that a moody-eyed, tattooed bad boy entered her domain. When their eyes met for the first time across the crowded, smoke-filled room, it really was as if the clichés had collided. Call it fate, destiny, or car-crash kismet, there can be no denying that unseen forces were at work that night. Though he'd surely have known already, he ambled over and asked Amy her name, and what she was drinking. And to paraphrase the Crystals' 1963 hit . . . then he kissed her.

*Love is a losing game: Amy and Blake in Toronto, Canada in May 2007, a few months before the full extent of their drug addiction became public knowledge.*

♪♪♪

It's fair to say that twenty-three-year-old music industry wannabe Blake Fielder-Civil's only claim to fame before becoming the poisoned apple of Amy's eye was that he'd worked as a 'go-fer' on a Lily Allen promo video shoot, in which he also had a cameo appearance handing Lily a rose. Indeed, saying he worked in the music industry was stretching credibility beyond its outer parameters. Like Amy, bad boy Blake came from a broken home. His father, Lance Fielder, a retired businessman, still lived in the London area, whereas his bohemian hairdresser mother, Georgette, who was some twenty-four years younger than Blake's father, was now living in Newark, Nottinghamshire, with her headmaster husband, Giles Civil, and their two teenage sons.

'One day she gets Blake tattooed on her chest,' was how Nick Godwyn recalled Amy's new love entering her life. 'Blake is on the scene and she changes. She might have changed because she had fallen in love with someone. People change when they are in love. She loved him. There's a different priority in life, I accepted that, but then other things started to change. Her behaviour became more erratic. She wasn't doing anything; not going away, not going into the studio. We arranged a trip for her to go to New York to meet the producer Mark Ronson and she wouldn't go.'

'One day she gets Blake tattooed on her chest . . .
Her behaviour became more erratic. She wasn't doing anything;
not going away, not going into the studio.' – Nick Godwyn

Blake was like the majority of wannabes wandering around Camden, in that he had no discernible talent of his own, and hoped that looking the part would get him the part – whatever the part might prove to be. Though Madonna and Guy Ritchie would cosy up with the locals at the Punch Bowl in Mayfair, it's not considered the norm for platinum-selling female singers to be seen letting their hair down and having a few bevvies in your average local low-rent boozer – especially without a team of perennially-shaded heavies sipping cokes at a nearby table. While sceptics will wonder whether Blake only started going into the Hawley Arms with an ulterior motive in mind – i.e. in the hope of finding Amy at the bar, catching her eye, and getting himself a gig – there's no arguing that he got more than he bargained for. But such was the immediate chemistry that first night that the pub's punters could have been forgiven for thinking Amy had been in there waiting for her beau.

'I spend a lot of time playing pool and listening to jukebox music,' she later told *Rolling Stone*, when asked to recount the events surrounding their first meeting. 'I used

*A youthful-looking Amy and Blake in 2005, before their first break-up,*
*which inspired Amy to write the majority of the songs on* Back to Black.

*If love is the drug: Amy and Blake backstage at the Coachella Festival in California, April 2007. Less than a month later, they were married.*

to smoke a lot of weed. I suppose if you have an addictive personality then you go from one poison to the other. He doesn't smoke weed, so I started drinking more and not smoking as much. And because of that I just enjoyed stuff more.'

The two soon became inseparable – like tattooed bookends. They would meet in the Hawley Arms each evening to drink some beers and shoot some pool, before heading out into the Camden night to continue their mutually exclusive party elsewhere – usually back at Amy's flat with the shades drawn. 'It was my second boyfriend, Blake, who kick-started my domestic instinct,' she later told the *Observer*. 'I immediately saw he was someone who hadn't been treated right, so I practically put him in my bag and said, "Right, you're coming with me!"'

That same month she also told *Totally Jewish*: 'Being Jewish to me is about being together as a real family. It's not about lighting candles and saying a bracha. In case you were wondering, Jewish men are off the agenda. I have a boyfriend who isn't Jewish, because most of the time I don't like Jewish men. I can't be doing with guys who have been smothered by their mothers.'

Their tumultuous relationship was all-consuming, with Amy thinking of little else but of spending every hour with her guy; not family, not friends, not even thinking about her career. Amy's drinking had already been bordering on excessive, but with Blake it began spiralling out of control. 'My justification is that most people my age spend a lot of their time thinking about what they're going to do for the next five or ten years,' she told the *Independent*. 'The time they spend thinking about

**'I'm either a really good drunk, or I'm an out-and-out shit, horrible, violent, abusive, emotional drunk.' – Amy Winehouse**

their life, I just spend drinking. I'm either a really good drunk, or I'm an out-and-out shit, horrible, violent, abusive, emotional drunk.' But they weren't only bonded by bourbon, and nights soaked in Jack'n'coke took on a whole new meaning. The girl who'd once eschewed hard drugs, and dismissed those who took them as 'arseholes', was now getting her thrills from assorted powders and pills. 'I shouldn't have been in a relationship with him [Blake],' she told the *Sun* in 2006. 'Because he was already with someone else a bit too close to home.'

For six months the romance raged, and had Amy met Blake before securing a recording contract with Island then it is likely that no one – other than her family and friends – would have given a toss, and left her and her new boyfriend to their own nefarious devices. But Amy was a platinum-selling artist, and there were too many people with vested interests in keeping her career on track, none of whom were willing to let a Camden chancer ruin things. Of course, hearing tales of external forces coming together to force young lovers apart, one is instantly reminded of the Montagues and Capulets colluding to separate Juliet from her beloved Romeo. And there's no denying that Amy and Blake's doomed romance had enough twists and turns for a Shakespearean yarn. Unable to cope with the pressures being exerted from all sides, the couple began taking their frustrations out on each other before finally going their separate ways. Blake sought succour in the arms of his seemingly forgiving ex-girlfriend, while Amy sought hers in the arms of Hawley. 'I was really depressed," she later told the *Daily Record*. 'I was in love with someone and it fell through. A lot of it was to do with bad choices and misgivings. We were both to blame for the split.'

But like all bad pennies, this one wouldn't stay lost down the back of the sofa for long.

♪ ♪ ♪

Though Amy had been wrenched away from her lover's arms, prising her from the bottle in which she was drowning her sorrows wasn't proving to be so easy. 'I was definitely drinking too much,' she told the *Daily Record* in 2006, shortly after *Back to Black* was released. 'I've always had a high tolerance for alcohol. The kind of states I was getting myself into was a joke. My friends would find me at six o'clock on a Saturday night drunk already. I shouldn't have been drunk at that time. I'd be wrecked from the day before, having stayed up all night and I'd still be up. Or I'd have passed out at five o'clock. It wasn't very healthy.' And while 'liquid lunches' are considered something of a norm in the entertainment world, those on liquid-only diets usually end up in the Priory, or the mortuary. And it wasn't as if the elfin singer had any surplus body fat to compensate for a lack of solids.

Indeed, Nick Godwyn, who hadn't seen much of Amy whilst she was out painting Camden lipstick-red with Blake, was shocked at how much weight she'd lost. 'I got a call from Nick [Shymansky]. "Come straight to Amy's,"' Nick explained. 'I get there and she is in pieces. It was shocking. I'd never seen her like that before. She was broken. She was crying, upset, saying she loves Blake. We were consoling her, but also said that maybe now is the time to talk to somebody.'

Nick was loath to use the word 'rehab' when he said that Amy should seek help, simply because it had such big connotations. He just wanted her to talk to someone. Amy's friends and neighbours agreed. The flat was in such a squalid state that once Mitch had come and collected Amy, her friends stayed behind to tidy up.

Though he and Nick Shymansky had worked so closely with Amy over the past six years, the hollow-eyed woman lying on the grubby couch was unrecognisable when compared to the rosy, vivacious teenager who had walked into their office back in 1999. They'd known that Amy's drinking had been steadily getting worse, and they'd both suspected that since meeting Blake, Amy had progressed from weed onto harder drugs. But neither they, nor anyone else close to Amy, realised just how far she had fallen.

'We did get her to the clinic,' Nick says. 'As the world now knows, it's all in the song, "Rehab". She didn't want to go but we knew it was the moment. We dropped her off, told her to call us, whatever she wanted was okay. Before we'd even sat down to have our lunch, she calls, "Right, done that." And so we took her back to London. What could we do?'

*Amy pauses for a sip of her drink during a performance*
*at Camden's Koko Club in November 2006.*

'It's too much of a drinking culture,' was Amy's explanation of her behaviour when speaking to the *Times* in 2006. 'Everything tastes better with a drink. Like, watch TV: glass of wine; cooking dinner: glass of champagne. I had a period where I struggled a little bit with eating disorders. It was only a year . . . only a few . . . I only really stopped it . . . The thing is, if you're an addict, you don't get over it, you're just in remission. So I won't sit here and go, "Yeah, I don't have a problem with food anymore." I do forget to eat a lot, and I do have my odd days where I think, "You can't eat because you ate that yesterday." But I think all modern girls are like that and I don't like to make too big a thing about it.'

Island, of course, wanted a follow-up album and had long been exerting external pressures of their own, eager to get Amy into a studio to work on new songs. So while her label bosses were undoubtedly pleased that Amy was committing her heartbreak to paper, they were less thrilled about the copious amount of spirits she was using as a mixer to aid her creative output. '*Back to Black* is when you've finished a relationship,' she told the *Sun* at the time of the album's release in 2006. 'And you go back to what's comfortable for you. My ex [Blake] went back to his girlfriend and I went back to drinking and dark times.'

> **'I was having a particularly nasty time with things and just drinking and drinking. My management decided to stop buying for me and said they were taking me to rehab.'** – Amy Winehouse

But rather than get involved with Amy's drinking problems directly, Island's head honchos let their anxieties be known at Brilliant's offices. And though Nick Godwyn saw himself as Amy's manager, and not her father, he had been forced to step in and suggest that Amy seek professional help. 'I was having a particularly nasty time with things and just drinking and drinking,' she told the *Sun* whilst explaining the inspiration behind the song with which she will forever be identified. 'My management decided to stop buying for me and said they were taking me to rehab. I asked my dad if he thought I needed to go. He said no [no, no], but I should give it a try. So I did, for just fifteen minutes. I went in, said "hello" and explained that I did drink because I am in love and have fucked up the relationship. Then I walked out.'

Another relationship about to go belly-up was the one between Amy and Nick Godwyn. 'After that [Amy's visit to the rehab centre], my relationship with her definitely changed,' Nick recounted in his piece for the *Times*. 'She wanted to go, didn't think she needed it and she lost her faith in me. My partner Nick moved on, and I was out of contract with Amy and nothing was happening. Eventually, we met in early 2005 and she was very quiet and very nice. I think she was dreading it, and she said she wanted a new manager. I made it easy for her. I understood why she was doing it. From sixteen to twenty-one, you change. I wasn't her character anymore and probably never was, really. I was Big Nick, Godders; I was older and maybe a bit sensible. And I'd seen it done too many times round the other way. I said to her, "I don't think you need a new manager, I think you need to make a record. You've got the best deals there have ever been." I said, "Send me the record when you make it because I'd like to hear it, because I'm a fan." But I'd also got pretty tired, and was possibly slightly relieved.'

In early 2006 Amy officially parted company with Brilliant and signed a new management deal with Raye Cosbert at Metropolis Music. Cosbert, who'd been with Metropolis since 1989, was already known to Amy, having promoted her post-*Frank* live shows. Aside from Amy, he'd also promoted the likes of Blur, Robbie Williams, Massive Attack and Iceland's diminutive diva, Björk. Having literally bumped into Amy on Camden High Street, and hearing that she was considering changing managers, he saw their chance encounter as a sign from above and readily offered his services.

It would take the best part of a year for Amy to make public her reasons for parting with Brilliant and signing with Cosbert. 'I was definitely unhappy with my management,' she told *CMU Beats Bar*. 'I was on a learning curve and through that I discovered I was with the wrong managers. Your management tend to be the go-between between you and your label, so because I was having problems with my managers I was going to have problems with the label. But most of those problems weren't really there. I didn't want to talk to my managers, which meant I never really spoke to the label, which probably meant they thought I was being awkward, that I didn't care. But now I've got the management thing fixed I get on brilliantly with my label.'

Island Records weren't overly concerned whose hand was on the tiller of Amy's ship as long as it remained anchored in their harbour. However, Guy Moot, the CEO at EMI Music Publishing, was particularly delighted at hearing the news. As he later told *Music Week*: 'Raye coming in put a real period of stability into the whole campaign. He is incredibly calm and by remaining calm, he focuses on what the goals are and at the same time harnesses the more erratic artistic moments that Amy has.'

♪ ♪ ♪

Aside from popping her head above the parapet to oversee the transference of the managerial reins, and her appearances at the Cornbury Music Festival the previous July, and a charity event at the Cobden Club in the November (her only live outings that year), Amy had been holed away inside her Camden enclave, feverishly writing the songs that would make up *Back to Black*. 'The songs I wrote on the album are from times when I was messed up in the head,' she told *Entertainment Weekly* in 2007. 'I had literally hit . . . not rock bottom, I hate to use such a phrase, since I'm sure I will sink lower at some point. But I was clinically depressed and I managed to get something

*If I can make it there, I'll make it anywhere: Amy at the launch of Kate Moss's TopShop range in New York, May 2007 (left), and (right) on the street in the same city four months later.*

I'm so proud of out of something that was so horrible.' Like a fabled tortured poet, it really did seem as though Amy was literally only on song when undergoing personal turmoil. 'I have to feel very strongly about something before I can write about it,' she told the *Sunday Herald* that same year whilst explaining her songwriting methods. 'But when I start, I'm on a roll. I am on a roll. This album [*Back to Black*] took me about six months to write. I guess someone reading this might think that was really long, but fuck you, it took me four years to write my first album.'

One day in early spring 2006, armed with Amy's latest outpourings set to verse and chorus, Cosbert walked into Darcus Beese's Island office to open negotiations on the long-awaited and much-anticipated second Amy Winehouse album. Cosbert had gone in there assuming that, with *Frank* having accrued platinum sales, Island would once again want Amy to team up with Salaam Remi and Commissioner Gordon. But although Remi's name was in the frame to oversee production on the entire album, Darcus Beese was keen for Amy to meet DJ and then up-and-coming New York-based producer, Mark Ronson. As Ronson also happened to be signed to EMI Music Publishing at the time, it's safe to assume that Ronson's name was being literally mooted around the corporate table by Guy Moot. In his aforementioned interview with *Music Week*, the EMI CEO cited Amy's signing with Raye Cosbert, and her subsequent collaboration with Mark Ronson as being the two pivotal moments in Amy's career.

'They [EMI] suggested we should work together, possibly because they were desperate to get something new out of me,' Amy told *CMU Beats Bar* in 2006. 'I wasn't too convinced at first. I kind of thought of Mark as some white guy who tried too hard. But we met, and he was much more friendly than I expected, and we had a lot more in common music-wise that I had thought. The record label [Island] had kept saying, "Do you want to make another album?" But I just wasn't ready. I had about three or four songs together, but that wasn't enough to get started properly. I only really got to that stage when I met Mark.'

> '**I had literally hit . . . not rock bottom, I hate to use such a phrase, since I'm sure I will sink lower at some point. But I was clinically depressed and I managed to get something I'm so proud of out of something that was so horrible.'** – Amy Winehouse

Music wasn't Amy and Ronson's only common ground. Like Amy, thirty-one-year-old Ronson had been born in London, was Jewish, and came from a broken home. When his mother remarried Mick Jones – the Hampshire-born guitarist with American AOR (Adult Oriented Rock) outfit Foreigner, who are perhaps best known for their 1981 hit 'Waiting for a Girl like You' – Ronson went with her to New York. Though he'd started out playing guitar in a local band, it was through switching to DJing on the Manhattan club scene that he began to accrue his reputation. His breakthrough as a producer came with working on Nikka Costa's 2001 album *Everybody's Got Their Something*, featuring the single 'Like a Feather', for which Ronson received a co-writer's credit. 2006 would prove a busy year for Ronson, as aside from his work on *Back to Black*, he also received production credits on Christina Aguilera's *Back to Basics*, Robbie Williams's *Rudebox*, and Lily Allen's 2006 triple platinum-selling *Alright, Still*. His work on the Nikka Costa album was enough to secure him a recording contract with Elektra Records, for whom he subsequently released his debut solo 2003 album, *Here Comes the Fuzz*, a multi-collaborative project that spawned the UK Top Twenty hit 'Ooh Wee', featuring Nate Dogg, Ghostface Killah, and Trife Da God. But while Guy Moot believes that Amy meeting Ronson was a pivotal point in her career, Ronson was quick to point out that the collaboration was mutually beneficial. 'I've always been really candid about saying that Amy is the reason I am on the map,' he said on *BBC Breakfast* in September 2010. 'If it wasn't for the success of *Back to Black*, no one would have cared too much about *Version* [Ronson's second album].'

'She [Amy] thought I was going to be some older Jewish guy or something,' Ronson told *Spin* magazine in July 2007. 'I don't know if she thought I'd be like Rick Rubin or maybe Leonard Cohen. We listened to everything, like Earl and the Cadillacs, and the Angels, and just started talking the way music geeks do when they get together. The reason everyone goes back to those Motown records is that there were amazing musicians playing together in a room, and that's what we tried to do.'

Like Amy, Ronson was an aficionado of sixties all-girl groups, and after their initial meeting he went into his studio to begin working on the song that would evolve into 'Back to Black', the album's title track. When they met up again the following afternoon, Amy was blown away by what Ronson had done and told him that was what she wanted the album to sound like. 'I'd play something I'd been working on, or a song I like, and then overnight he'd think about it and come back to me with an idea or suggestion or another song he liked,' Amy enthused to *CMU Beats Bar*. 'Once me and Mark started doing that stuff I was ready to start work on a new album, and that's what we spent the first half of the year doing.'

One of the first songs they worked on together was 'Rehab'. According to Ronson, who was expounding upon the songwriting process during an interview with Radio One DJ Zane Lowe for the station's documentary series *Stories*, first broadcast on Monday, 18 July 2011, the song was literally one of those off-the-cuff, spur-of-the-moment things. 'We were in New York,' he told Zane. 'We'd been working together for about a week and we were walking to some store. She wanted to buy a present for her boyfriend [Blake] and she was telling me about a specific time in her life that was . . . I feel bad, like, talking about a friend like this, but I think I've told this story enough times . . . but she hit, like, a certain low and her dad came over to try and talk some sense into her. And she was like, "He tried to make me go to rehab, and I was like, pfft, no, no, no." And the first thing I was like, ding-ding-ding. Like, I mean, I'm supposed to be like, "How was that for you?" and all I'm like is, "We've got to go back to the studio."'

'Me and Mark Ronson were just walking down the street in SoHo, and I sang the hook. I sang it as a joke,' was how Amy herself explained the song's origins to *Papermag*. 'Mark started laughing, saying, "That's so funny. That's so funny, Amy. Whose song is that, man?" I told him, "I just wrote it off the top of my head. I was just joking." And he said, "It would be so cool if you had a whole song about rehab." I said, "Well, I could write it right now. Let's go to the studio." And that was it.'

Though Nick Godwyn says he was responsible for Amy going into rehab – even if it was for all of five minutes – when talking to the *Sunday Tribune* in 2007, Amy would give a different version of the events that would ultimately lead to her first UK Top Ten single. In this version it was Amy's old flame, Tyler James, who acted as the catalyst for her seeing a counsellor. 'We were so close that he [Tyler] did so

*Amy walks the streets of London's Soho with her old friend Tyler James, who was responsible for introducing her to her first management team, September 2009.*

much for me for nothing, and I love him and respect that,' she said. 'He's still like my big brother. I think he was at the end of his rope. After the end of a particularly nasty drunken episode he called my dad who said, "You gotta come and see me and stay a couple of days." So I said, "Okay, I'll come and stay."' Once Amy was out of harm's way and under Mitch's roof, he and Tyler made the appointment for her to be assessed for possible dependency issues, and how they might best be treated.

'I walked in and the guy said, "Why do you think you are here?" I said, "I am drinking a lot, I'm in love and I fucked it up, and I'm a manic depressive." I didn't want to say no because he might think I was in denial. He started talking and I kinda switched off and fifteen minutes later I went, "Thanks very much." I genuinely believe that if you can't sort yourself out no one else can. Afterwards, I asked my dad, "Do you think I need to go to rehab, really?" And he said, "No."'

> **'Sometimes I start with a sentiment but other times I might start with some lyrics or a melody in my head, and then musical chords on the guitar are usually the last thing I add.'**
> – Amy Winehouse

When Amy wasn't in New York with Ronson she'd be in Miami at Salaam Remi's home studio, laying down the basic tracks for his half of the album. To capture the vintage sound Amy was looking for, Remi studied the techniques of legendary Atlantic engineer Tom Dowd, and got in touch with Jim Gaines, a former sound engineer at Stax Records, to pick his brains about the methods he'd used back in the day, as well as ask for Gaines's opinion on how best to recreate that telltale crackly vinyl sound. Armed with this information, Remi had Amy singing in the living room while recording her from an upstairs bedroom. 'The songs were twisted around that format in the same tempo and were lyrically all the same,' he told *Remix* magazine. 'What pulls the album together is Amy's confidence and what she wanted to hear.'

What Amy was hearing in the clutch of songs she'd already written was the haunting sound of teenage heartbreak that had drifted out from the Hawley Arms jukebox while she and Blake were living out their own minor-chord melodrama. 'I wrote my first album when I was listening to a lot of jazz, a lot of hip-hop,' she told *Entertainment Weekly* in 2007. 'When I listen to my second album, I was listening to a substantially smaller amount of music – soul, doo-wop, girl groups – and it shows. I was just listening to very different types of music when I did two different albums.' And just like the fictional ne'er-do-wells emotively brought to life by Ronnie Spector, Betty Weiss, Shirley Owens, et al, Amy had her own bad boy to guide her hand.

'I suppose I start with a sentiment, but that sounds a bit cheesy, doesn't it?' she told the *Mail Online* whilst explaining her songwriting technique in August 2007. 'Sometimes I start with a sentiment but other times I might start with some lyrics or a melody in my head, and then musical chords on the guitar are usually the last thing I add.'

Meanwhile Mark Ronson, having realised which musical direction Amy was taking with the majority of her new songs, cast himself as a Phil Spector to Remi's Berry Gordy Jr, and to bring the doo-wop/soul hybrid together he brought in the Dap-Kings, a nine-piece house band working out of Daptones Studio in Brooklyn, to add their seventies funk/soul vibe to the mix. Another Brooklyn-based musician brought in by Ronson was Victor 'Ticklah' Axelrod, who coincidentally had also worked with the Dap-Kings. But whereas the Dap-Kings' not insignificant contributions to the album would largely go unheralded, Axelrod would be credited for his piano and Wurlitzer work on songs such as 'Rehab', 'Love Is a Losing Game', 'Some Unholy War', and 'Back to Black'. 'I remember the demo of "Back to Black",' Axelrod says today. 'We listened to the demo and sort of set a vibe from that. It had a Phil Spector feel. I remember being really pleasantly surprised at how much I liked the songs while listening to the demos with Amy's voice.'

A couple of thousand miles further down the Atlantic coast in Miami, Remi had once again called on the services of Troy Genius. '*Back to Black* was basically the same [as making *Frank*] because Amy had the same jazzy feel, so it really wasn't all that different on the second album,' Genius says. 'We just sat in the studio and we listened to it and we talked about what kind of feel, what kind of ideas. And then I'd go in there and do about four or five different types of stuff and we'd take whichever one worked best.'

As with all the other projects they'd collaborated on over the years, Remi and Genius worked alone. And such was their understanding of what each required of the other that Remi's directions tended to be abstract rather than figurative. 'Salaam was always mentioning a grainy feel with a little red and a little orange,' Genius says. 'All those textures have a definite meeting. An orangey red is more of a warm feeling. Grainy means that it has a little edge to it. He knows how to get to that final product.'

On listening to the final product back in London, Darcus Beese knew Amy had surpassed herself. He also knew teaming her and Remi up with the more pop-oriented Mark Ronson had been the right way to proceed. *Frank* was a very good album, whereas the follow-up – brimming with songs that had 'single' written all over them – was promising to be a great album.

# 6. That Ol' Back to Black Magic

'Music is the only thing I have with real dignity in my life. That's the one area in my life where I can hold my head up and say, "No one can touch me."'

Though a headline ten-date UK tour to promote *Back To Black* was set to commence at the Liverpool Academy 2 on Friday 10 November, it had been nigh on ten months since Amy had last performed in front of a live audience. As a means of dusting off the cobwebs – as well as a chance to showcase the new material prior to the album's release – three warm-up dates over consecutive nights were arranged, starting in Bristol at the Fleece on Sunday 10 September. It wasn't only the new material that was unveiled that evening, as the slim-lined Amy – decked out in suitably figure-hugging attire – was sporting a stacked-up beehive and Cleopatra make-up that her new stylist, Alex Foden, had clearly borrowed from Ronnie Spector during her Ronettes heyday. Amy's imitation was apparently so startling that New York's *Village Voice* subsequently reported: 'Ronnie Spector – who, it could be argued, all but invented Winehouse's style in the first place when she took the stage at the Brooklyn Fox Theatre with her fellow Ronettes more than forty years ago – was so taken aback at a picture of Winehouse in the *New York Post* that she exclaimed, "I don't know her, I never met her, and when I saw that picture, I thought, that's me! But then I found out, no, it's Amy! I didn't have on my glasses."'

In its review of the Bristol show, the *Daily Telegraph* gave up as much – if not more – copy to Amy's weight loss and her Ronnie Spector-esque makeover as it did to her performance on the night. 'Overall, the music is still less interesting than Winehouse herself. She's even more striking than before.' After noting that Amy's new waiflike appearance was –somewhat inevitably – being scrutinised by all the celebrity magazines, the paper found itself asking the question on everyone's lips:

*Every rose has its thorn: Amy at the South Bank Show Awards in January 2007.*

how was it that a voice so colossal could possibly emanate from a girl who looked as if a stiff breeze would blow her from the stage?

The *Independent* was also in attendance, and expressed its unwavering support of Amy's transition from curvy teenager to (alleged) emaciated fitness addict by saying, 'It's not enough to be a pop star nowadays – you have to be a victim too.' And though the paper was prepared to mention Amy's messing up the lyrics on some of the new songs, it was quick to point out that she did so with carefree abandon.

Perhaps unsurprisingly, given that the Bristol show was Amy's first live performance for the best part of a year, and the first time songs from the forthcoming album were given a public airing, neither review was particularly enthusiastic in its comments about Amy's performance; a pattern that was to be repeated by Brighton's local paper, the *Argus*, when casting its critical eye over Amy's show at the Concorde 2 the following evening. Though the review was at least appreciative of the new material, it was equally critical of Amy's onstage efforts. 'She seemed self-consciously disembodied from her old songs and fluffed her lines more than a couple of times.'

> **Penning songs such as 'Love Is a Losing Game' and 'Back to Black' was set to cost Amy heavily, as she would now have to relive the anguish of her split from Blake every night – in front of an audience.**

Though she'd spent six months in the studio recording the new songs, Amy was out of live practice, which perhaps explains the somewhat cool reception afforded the new material. But, like the *Independent* the previous night, the *Argus* was in a benevolent mood, and put the glitches down to Amy being shy because boyfriend Alex Jones-Donelly was in the audience.

Amy's final warm-up show was at the Bloomsbury Ballroom in London and the *Guardian* was there to welcome her home in style. Although it would have been remiss of the paper not to mention Amy's new svelte frame, the review concentrated primarily on the performance. 'Winehouse's issues are the fulcrum of her music and the emotions they provoke seep into her smoke-stained voice.' This, as the paper rightly pointed out, was Amy's primary selling point – her unnerving ability to transform her failings in love into songs that stirred the emotions. The review also made note of how Amy's vocal style had acquired subtlety in the three years since *Frank*. Where once she had perhaps been guilty of belting out the songs as if to batter her audience into sonic submission, she had since learnt how to tease and caress, and her performance was all the better for it.

While all the reviews waxed lyrical about the new material on *Back to Black* being of an autobiographical nature, and how Amy was allowing us a sneaky-peak through the keyhole to her blues-embittered soul, what they seemingly failed to pick up on was that penning songs such as 'Love Is a Losing Game', 'Tears Dry on Their Own' and 'Back to Black' was set to cost Amy heavily, as she would now have to relive the anguish of her split from Blake every night – in front of an audience.

♪ ♪ ♪

If *Frank* had been considered something of a slow-burner at Island HQ, then in the week following its release in early October 2006, *Back to Back* slammed into the unsuspecting UK album chart like a souped-up Scud missile. In its first week alone the album shifted 43,000 copies, and by the end of the year had been certified platinum. Then, having claimed the coveted number 1 spot in the week ending 20 January 2007 – a feat that would be repeated several times over throughout the remainder of the year, from January through to July – it would spend twenty-seven consecutive weeks in the Top Ten. But the Amy epidemic showed little sign of abating in the run-up to the second Christmas since its release, and by the time she appeared onstage with Paul Weller on Jools Holland's Hogmanay *Hootenanny*, *Back to Black* had been certified five-times platinum in the UK by the British Phonographic Institute in recognition of over 1.8 million units sold. Owing to the album's phenomenal success, *Frank* re-entered the UK chart at number 22 in February 2007, and became something of a mainstay throughout the remainder of the year.

The new album's change in musical direction was matched by a visual transformation evident in its cover shot. Gone was the girl about town out walking her dog, and in her place sat a brooding alter-ego who stared nonchalantly into the camera, as though daring us to draw conclusions.

Not surprisingly, the UK media went into overdrive in its eulogising of both Amy and the album. The *Times* proclaimed *Back to Black* to be 'another record redolent with the tang of modern bohemia, building on the platinum-selling *Frank*'s witty exploration of sex and self-realisation', while the *Daily Telegraph* said that with the album Amy was 'slamming the door on those laidback lounge influences and strutting into a gloriously ballsy, bell-ringing, bottle-swigging, doo-wop territory'. The *Observer* hailed cited *Back to Black* as 'a starkly confessional album, chiffon-light in parts as it is unflinching in others', while the *NME* cited the album as a 'tapestry of undeniable musical brilliance'.

Indeed, the response was so positive that even those glossy gossip columnists who had been sniping at Amy since her break-up with Blake the previous year were forced to sit up and take notice.

*Back to Black* is undoubtedly influenced by the sensibilities of 1960s pop and soul. Remi and Ronson's twin attack serves to bring Amy's tales to life in a stirring mélange of Muscle Shoals and Funk Brothers-driven Motown. Thematically, Amy wanders through girl-group territory, making explicit the anguish of heartache that the

Supremes only ever hinted at, while at the same time displaying the sort of vocal depth that most singers can only dream of. The album's compelling melodies provide a late-1950s, *American Graffiti*-esque backdrop, while Amy assumes the role of a chanteuse bemoaning her experiences in modern-day London. As if to emphasise just how worldly-wise she has become in so short a time, Amy seems to have purposely kept each track to around the length of an old jukebox 45, which enables her to make her point and move on without running the risk of outstaying her welcome.

'Rehab', the much-vaunted opening number, comes across like an obscure northern soul gem, riddled with pathos and melodrama. In fact, none of the music here sounds like it was made after 1967. 'Rehab' isn't your typical pop song, but of course, Amy isn't your typical pop singer. While she's happy to bemoan her problems, she doesn't give a toss what the rest of us think of them. And while it could be argued that Island were subliminally highlighting Amy's spiralling drink and drug problems by selecting 'Rehab' and 'Addicted' to open and close the album, it's also worth remembering that nothing sells quite like sincerity.

> **With its classic minor-chord Motown piano, tambourine taps, and jaunty bass rhythm, the riveting title track 'Back to Black' is classic Supremes meets Dame Shirley Bassey.**

Track two, 'You Know I'm No Good', begins with a classic mid-sixties soul beat, highly reminiscent of Otis Redding and Carla Thomas's 'Tramp', before slowly evolving into a tale of infidelity and betrayal, in which our heroine's lover spots telltale 'likkle carpet burns' while she's taking a bath. 'Me and Mr Jones' opens with a classic doo-wop backing chorus as provided by the Dap-Kings, before slipping into a stomping rhythm of jangly guitars and Tamla-esque tambourines. The 'Me' in the title is clearly Amy, while the enigmatic 'Mr Jones' is the hapless boyfriend who falls foul of her rant after – amongst his other failings – standing her up so that she misses a show by the rapper Slick Rick.

The Specials-esque 'Just Friends', with its glorious reggae beat held down by Troy Genius, is perhaps the only track on *Back to Black* that wouldn't have sounded out of place on *Frank*. And as such, serves as a reminder of where Amy has come from musically. With its classic minor-chord Motown piano, tambourine taps, and jaunty bass rhythm, the riveting title track 'Back to Black' is classic Supremes meets Dame Shirley Bassey. Indeed, it could be said that it's the best James Bond theme tune never made, while Amy's haunting lyric 'you go back to her, and I go back to black' – her most poignant reference to her break-up with Blake – recalls the foreboding atmosphere of the Shangri-La's 'Remember (Walking in the Sand)'.

*Amy adopted a classic sixties Bond girl look for this performance of 'Rehab' at the MTV Movie Awards, held in Los Angeles in June 2007.*

'Love Is a Losing Game', with its sultry piano, soft bass, and clipped guitar, is undoubtedly the sweetest-sounding track on the album. The Dap-Kings come into their own here, and provide a sublime seventies soul feel over which Amy's understated lyric brims with regret – as if she's trying to explain why she's stayed with the guy who's repeatedly done her wrong. 'Tears Dry on Their Own' recasts the spirit of its instantly recognizable source material, 'Ain't No Mountain High Enough' (the original Marvin Gaye and Tammi Terrell duet). Sampling a beloved soul classic is usually a dangerous move, but when executed with strokes of innovation, the results give sampling a good name. Here, the song is an ode to Winehouse's independence, even though her heart is broken. In contrast to Marvin Gaye's soaring vocal, Winehouse flips the melody in the verses so that it descends rather than ascends. The way she spits out the syllables of 'inevitable' conveys a forced admission that she might be better off without her man. She's walking away, yet compelled to stop and glance over her shoulder as she goes. 'I don't listen to a lot of new stuff,' she told *Spin* magazine the following year when *Back to Black* was laying siege to the album charts on both sides of the Atlantic. 'I just like the old stuff . . . you'd have an entire story in a song. I never listen to, like, white music – I couldn't sing you a Zeppelin or Floyd song. I write songs because I . . . need to get something good out of something bad. I thought, "Fuck, I'm going to die if I don't write down the way I feel."'

'Wake Up Alone' is another three-minute vignette of romantic angst which dissects the angst of waking up and going through the day without that special someone who was once a constant presence, while Amy's vocal phrasing on 'He Can Only Hold Her' shows her at her best.

'Some Unholy War' is a mish-mash of musical styles over a calypso beat, and as a result is perhaps the weakest song on the album. As previously mentioned, *Back to Black* closes with 'Addicted', an ode to the delights of weed laid over a pumping Miles Davis-goes-to-Motown beat, in which Amy berates her friend's boyfriend for smoking all her 'home-grown' and reveals her own excesses where the drug is concerned.

In its retrospective souvenir issue following Amy's death, the *NME* said: 'If for no other reason than for helping to establish an entire cottage industry of retro-soul jazz divas, *Back to Black* can be considered one of the most influential albums of the past ten years. It is also, however, unquestionably one of the best.' After first lauding *Frank* as having been a 'serviceable introduction' to Amy's talents, the paper credited *Back to Black* for having raised the bar for mid-noughties pop music, and 'going on to become one of those rare albums that is both stupidly successful and richly deserving of it'.

The retrospective piece also observed that Amy's songwriting talents were all too often underrated, and that in contrast to her 'heavily co-written debut', every track on *Black to Black* was 'imbued with her own insecurities, contradictions and self-loathing to create something genuinely – perhaps even uncomfortably – real, true and soulful'. The review was also astute in acknowledging that even the most cursory of listens to Amy's vocal on songs such as 'Love Is a Losing Game' and 'Tears Dry on Their Own' reveals an anguish and despair in the delivery that is utterly and heartrendingly authentic.

♪ ♪ ♪

It was in the week leading up to *Back to Black*'s release that the *NME* conducted its first interview with Amy whilst out on what the intrepid, cast-iron-stomached interviewer, Krissi Murison – later promoted to editor – later described as a 'short crawl of Camden's many dingy bar-rooms'.

'In the three years since becoming the nation's second favourite jazz warbler,' Murison writes, 'the girl formerly known as "the one who isn't Katie Melua" has undergone quite a transformation [. . .] resplendent in her trademark war-paint make-up, necking jugs of cocktails, and sporting a huge, naked woman tattoo on her arm, she's every bit the outrageous pop icon that makes Lily Allen look like Mother Teresa.'

> **'I write songs because I . . . need to get something good out of something bad. I thought, "Fuck, I'm going to die if I don't write down the way I feel."' – Amy Winehouse**

After lauding the merits of 'Rehab', and highlighting the problems that led to its creation, including Amy's penchant for binge-drinking, and her being diagnosed as a manic-depressive a year and a half earlier, Ms Murison still found Amy to be 'dazzling company, ferociously funny, and despite rumours about a figure-ravishing eating disorder, startlingly attractive'. With a new boyfriend, and a new management team to go with her new album, the upbeat Amy was more than happy to divulge details about any subject imaginable – ranging from a tongue-in-cheek response to a question about her favourite drug, through to her rectifying a recent tabloid tale in which she supposedly launched a candlestick at a gatecrasher at her birthday party. 'It wasn't a gatecrasher, it was my boyfriend,' she responds candidly, 'and it wasn't a candlestick, it was a bottle of Jack Daniel's.'

During the course of the pub crawl, Amy proved herself to be something of an authority on music, eulogising about Johnny Cash one minute, skanking along to the ska selections she'd made on the jukebox the next. She revealed that Pete Doherty – whom she apparently first encountered on a TV show – asked her to duet some Billie Holiday songs with him ('It never happened, but it still might'), and that she liked the Zutons (the Liverpool indie combo who penned 'Valerie', which Amy would subsequently record with Mark Ronson), but had accidentally told their singer Dave McCabe to fuck off at a party once. That four-letter faux pas, coupled with Amy's tattoos, talent, and unruly behaviour, was enough to give her some serious rock'n'roll credibility in the *NME*'s eyes.

*Amy's dramatic weight loss is increasingly visible backstage in Chicago in August 2007 (left), and (right) Amy gazes up at Blake, who watched her May 2007 Shepherd's Bush Empire show from a balcony above the stage.*

The new man who Amy was alluding to in the *NME* interview was Alex Jones-Donelly, who'd recently quit his high-powered job at EMI Music Publishing to become a chef. He and Amy had started seeing each other in June. Prior to being headhunted by Guy Moot, Jones-Donelly had spent seven years as Head of Music and Live Music at Radio One. 'If I'm checking out a man I'll usually go for someone who is at least five nine, with dark hair, dark eyes and loads of tattoos,' she told the *Observer*. 'But saying that, my current boyfriend is the most beautiful man I've ever seen in my life, and he's blonde, so I guess it doesn't matter that much. I just like a man who I can muck about with, and who can take a joke. I admire men who don't take anything seriously, like Dean Martin, who had this amazing ability to distance people from himself. He never talked about troubles with his marriage and would have a line for everything. Also Sammy Davis Jr, who treated all that racism like water off a duck's back. He was like, "Fuck it, I've got music." That's how I feel.'

It would seem that recording *Back to Black* had proved most cathartic for Amy, and now that she'd found a new man, and exorcised the ghost of boyfriends past from her mind, she joined a gym and took up exercising for real.

'The papers go on about how I lost weight, but I didn't notice myself losing it,' she told the *Observer*. 'I used to smoke £200 worth of weed a week, that's two ounces, which is disgusting, and it made me eat crap food on impulse. I lost the weight when I stopped smoking weed and got into the gym instead. I like my gym because there are all these sweaty men around to gear me up and get my adrenaline going. You want to sweat and look good. When I'm in a women's gym and they see me in my standard make-up, the women look at you as if to say, "Who are you trying to impress?" At the men's gym it's like, "Run girl, run!" I don't mind being looked at by men, I'm competitive.'

Yet according to an article that appeared in the *Daily Mail*, which was also delving into the reasons for Amy's drastic weight loss between albums, Amy had joined Fitness First, a women-only gym in Chalk Farm. If the article was to be believed, Amy was in there practically every afternoon undergoing a strict workout regime under watchful supervision of a personal trainer. When quoting from their own anonymous source, the *Mail* speculated that Amy was self-conscious about the media attention over her image, and that while she didn't mind people criticising her music, she'd been devastated by the snide remarks about her appearance that were appearing in the press on a near-daily basis. Yet Amy herself would tell the *Guardian*: 'I don't want to be the prettiest or the sexiest. I just want to look different and to look like me.'

♪ ♪ ♪

With *Back to Black* nestled in the album chart's top three, Amy's enthusiastic gym-going wouldn't have been the only thing making her feel good. She might still have been eschewing tabloid reviews – even though said reviews were radiating superfluity – but if Island's in-house calculations were correct, then some 70,000 souls had stepped out of their respective daily routine to purchase a copy of the album in its first two weeks of release. But all her hard work and newly-earned kudos was overshadowed by her shambolic appearance on *The Charlotte Church Show*, alongside ex-Atomic Kitten and reality-TV star Kerry Katona, Welsh comedian Rhod Gilbert, and Lily Allen's actor dad, Keith, which was aired on Channel 4 on Friday 13 October. For those of a superstitious nature, Friday falling on the thirteenth day of the month held ominous portents, and though the late-night chat show was recorded on the Wednesday afternoon, it was certainly an ill-omened outing for Amy.

In what was a blatant two-fingered snub to her Island bosses' pleas for her to curb her drinking, Amy reportedly began the day with a champagne breakfast – forgetting to have the accompanying meal – then moved onto a liquid lunch with a generous side-order of top-shelf optics, which carried on until the car arrived to ferry her to the television studio on the South Bank. Upon arrival, she was allowed to quaff her way through whatever was on offer in the green room before staggering onto the set, and what was seen by all at Island as a gilt-edged opportunity for Amy to plug her album to middle England's armchair masses rapidly descended into car-crash television. Not only did Amy struggle with the autocue, and constantly thrust her face into shot while the bemused Church – who is no lilting lily of the valley herself – tried talking to her other guests, she also smashed her foot into a glass table when getting up to perform a duet with the bemused host. But the pièce de risible résistance came with her repeatedly fluffing the lyrics to Michael Jackson's 1983 hit 'Beat It'.

Back in 2004, Amy had told the *Guardian* how she'd been a huge fan of Jackson's, and had then gone on to defend her shamed hero to the hilt following the accusations of child abuse that all but ended the self-styled King of Pop's career. One can almost imagine a pre-teen Amy – all pigtails and rosy cheeks – miming along to Jacko's songs in front of the bedroom mirror, her hairbrush serving as a microphone. Now here she was being invited to perform what was one of his best-known songs as a duet with Charlotte Church on primetime terrestrial TV. Whatever your opinions of Michael Jackson as a person, no one can deny the guy was a genius when it came to music, and both the studio audience and the viewers at home must have been thrilled at the prospect of having two of the most exciting female vocalists around belting out a Jackson classic. Church, who is classically trained, and can hold a note

> **'I went through every eating disorder you can have. A little bit of anorexia, a little bit of bulimia. I'm not totally okay now but I don't think any woman is.'** – Amy Winehouse

longer than a politician can hold a grudge, gave the song her all, while Amy sounded like Catherine Tate's character Lauren 'Am I bovvered?' Cooper after a night on the alcopops. Church, of course, has been known to knock 'em back herself on occasion, but even she was taken aback by Amy's total lack of professionalism. She later told *Contactmusic*: 'Amy kept forgetting the words. I told her, "When I squeeze you, it's your turn to sing." We did it with me poking her in the back.'

By all accounts, it took Amy three attempts to nail the song, and one can only begin to imagine what the audience's reaction was each time the producer yelled, 'Cut!' Indeed, one wonders why the beleaguered producer didn't simply give up the ghost after the second failure to launch and either have Church sing the song herself, or edit out the duet and replace it with the promo video for 'Rehab', which would have been rather fitting given the circumstances. Amy probably went home, slept off her drinking binge, and woke the following morning with little or no recollection of what had gone the day before. But if that was the case, then the tabloid headlines that morning would have served as an unsavoury reminder.

'Amy Wino – Singer Drunk for Charlotte Church TV Chat Show' decried the *Daily Mirror*, echoing back to its 'The Filth and the Fury' headline following the Sex

*A frail-looking Amy performs at the Virgin Festival in Baltimore, August 2007.*

Pistols' now-infamous appearance on the *Today* show some three decades earlier. 'It takes a lot to upstage earthy Charlotte Church and veteran hell-raiser Keith Allen,' said the *Mirror*'s intrepid reporter. 'But Amy Winehouse managed to do just that with her shambolic appearance on the Welsh star's chat show.' The story then offered a veiled hint at Amy's drink problem by saying how the 'smoky-voiced singer' had been 'tired and emotional' during the recording. But of course, once the tabloids get their fangs into a story they keep sucking until the victim has been blanched. And on the following Monday, the *Mirror* carried another story about how Amy's bosses at Island were becoming increasingly concerned that her public reputation for drinking was beginning to overshadow her singing, and that they'd advised Amy to tone down her drinking prior to her TV appearance. The paper then fell back on the disclaimer used by journalists everywhere by quoting an 'anonymous' label insider as saying, 'Amy is a vibrant character and the record company love the fact that she's got spirit, but her consumption of alcohol is seriously getting out of hand. She's turning up to interviews out of her head and she usually sinks more booze while being grilled about her life. We're all worried that she's going off the rails. She's been told that if she doesn't curb things she will have to go into rehab to sort herself out.'

> **'What can I say? I'm an insecure person. I'm very insecure about the way I look. I mean, I'm a singer, not a model. The more insecure I felt, the more I drank.'** – Amy Winehouse

Even if the insider existed anywhere other than the *Mirror* reporter's fertile imagination, he or she would hardly have been hauled over the coals for talking to the press, because it was basically free publicity for the soon-to-be-released 'Rehab' single. The edition also carried a quote from Amy in which she confessed to having an eating disorder. 'I went through every eating disorder you can have,' she said. 'A little bit of anorexia, a little bit of bulimia. I'm not totally okay now but I don't think any woman is.'

Though the *Mirror*'s copy had undoubtedly dented her public image, it certainly hadn't done any harm sales wise, as *Back to Black* was flying off the shelves in record shops and department stores up and down the country. To show she bore no ill will towards the paper, Amy later gave an exclusive interview in which she openly discussed being diagnosed with manic depression, and her flying visit to a rehab centre. 'I had to go to rehab to find out what it was like but it's not for me,' she explained. 'It would only increase my anxieties. I was always prone to depression but I didn't realise how much. I was on anti-depressants and the pill when I was younger, but the hormones go crazy and it drove me mad. Creative people shouldn't be on anti-depressants or any drugs.'

The *NME* had cited the recently released 'Rehab' as being a 'hip-sashaying homage to sixties girl-groups like the Supremes and the Shangri-Las, sung through the pipes of Aretha Franklin and the liver of Janis Joplin'. And of course, given what eventually happened, the Janis Joplin allusion was particularly resonant. 'It's completely autobiographical. I was drinking too much . . . about twenty units a day,' she told the paper. 'Anyway, my mates came round at about 10:00am; I was passed out on the floor with an empty bottle of Jack Daniel's in my hand. My house was a mess – blood, vomit, spunk up the walls. They [her concerned mates] burned all my clothes! The next morning my managers came round and said, "There's this place we wanna take you." I was like, "Okay mate, let me put my face on and have a fucking bath first, bastards!"'

♪ ♪ ♪

On Monday 23 October, with the parent album laying siege to the album chart, Island released 'Rehab' backed with 'Do Me Good' as the first single from *Back to Black*. Like the song it was promoting, the cover shot – of Amy looking very seductive with her Cher-esque corkscrew tresses tumbling down about her shoulders, and sporting a sexy white knee-length raincoat cinched at the waist as she eases past an ensemble of black musicians on a stairwell – is a world removed from the babysitter/girl-next-door imagery of the *Frank*-era covers. Like Ronson's retro, yet here-in-the-now, Spector-esque wall-of-sound heard at the song's intro, the imagery is pure vintage Americana. This is no longer a girl to take home to mum; this is a woman who isn't going to be taken anywhere unless she's already heading in that direction. The cover shot for the alternate format, which included a remix of 'Rehab' featuring the rapper Jay Z, was even more risqué. Amy, in all her pompadour glory, sits perched on the edge of a sofa within a fifties period living room glancing beyond the camera, while sporting a revealing black silky camisole. 'Rehab' would finally see Amy live up to her potential as the single crashed into the UK chart at number 19 on download sales alone, before then making its steady ascent up the rankings to number 7 following the CD's release.

Yet despite her continuing success, Amy continued to be plagued by insecurities, and it seemed the only way she could be certain of banishing her anxieties – at least for an evening –was to drown them in vodka. 'What can I say, I'm an insecure person,' she later told the *Daily Mail* when everyone began to believe Amy was only seeing glimpses of daylight through the bottom of the bottle. 'I'm very insecure about the way I look. I mean, I'm a singer, not a model. The more insecure I felt, the more I drank.'

Of course, her insecurities were merely exacerbated by *Back to Black*'s continuing success. It was as if she was loath to be seen basking in her glory, regardless of said glory being wholly deserved. 'I don't care about any of this, and I don't have much of an opinion of myself,' she told *Spin* magazine in 2007. 'I don't think people care about me . . . I made an album I'm very proud of and that's about it.'

# 7. The Girl Can't Help It

'I don't have many morals. My boyfriend is going, "You cheated on me," and I go, "Well, I told you I was a good for nothing."'

When Amy arrived in Liverpool on Friday, 10 November for the opening night of her headline tour at the city's Academy 2, she did so under something of a cloud, owing yet again to her feckless nature. Whilst attending the seventeenth annual Q Awards ceremony at the Grosvenor House Hotel in London eleven days earlier, she'd brazenly heckled U2's Bono by shouting, 'Shut up! I don't give a fuck!' when he'd been up at the podium giving a speech, after he and his fellow Irish rockers had collected the highly-prestigious, one-time-only Q Award of Awards: Band of Bands accolade for polling the most votes from Q readers through the awards' seventeen-year history. Of course, the more gauche amongst the audience thought her outburst hilarious, but the vast majority of attendees inwardly cringed and sat staring uncomfortably into space while the tumbleweeds rolled across the room. For though rebellious behaviour has come to be expected from young pretenders, dues have to be paid to those who have gone before and lasted the distance. It matters not a jot that U2 perhaps weren't the creative powerhouses they once were, or that Bono had delusions of political grandeur way above his station – they had a mighty impressive canon of work, and were still capable of filling arenas, while Amy had just released her second album, and was playing the sort of venues that hadn't hosted a U2 show in the past twenty years or more.

Back in 1975, a certain John Lydon (soon to be rechristened 'Johnny Rotten') was deemed suitably outré enough to be the fledgling Sex Pistols' frontman for sporting a Pink Floyd t-shirt on which he'd scrawled the words 'I Hate'. Of course, these days such sartorial posturing would be considered satirical rather than sacrilegious,

*Mellow yellow: Amy works the red carpet at the 2007 Brit Awards, wearing a striking mini-dress that became one of her favourites.*

but knowing that her detractors were poised waiting in anticipation of her making another vodka-fuelled faux pas, Amy thought she'd blunt their poisoned quills by offering 'I Hate Amy Winehouse' t-shirts as part of her official tour merchandise.

Liverpool, of course, is almost as famous for its comedians as its musicians, and the Scousers coming through the Academy's doors and seeing the t-shirts on display immediately understood the intended irony behind Amy's self-deprecating statement of intent. Indeed, the *Liverpool Echo*'s Johnny-on-the-spot thought it amusing enough to open his review. 'The £12-a-throw t-shirts provide as good an introduction to the mindset of the hardy and veracious soul-rider, as the slow climbing jazz/lounge backdrop coupled with life-bearing vocals of the opener, "Know You Now".' The review also made note of the venue being way too big for the occasion, and that as a result the subtle chord changes and tempo waves were largely lost and struggled to make an impact. Though each number was rapturously received in turn, it was the new single 'Rehab' – which according to the *Echo* had 'raised her profile to Jonathan Ross levels' – that received the biggest cheer of the evening.

> **'I also got sent to food rehab, and that was exactly the same as the alcohol one. I walked in and was like, "I don't need this," and walked straight back out.' – Amy Winehouse**

Following on from another sell-out show at Leeds Wardrobe on the 11 November, Amy headed up to Glasgow to play the 400-capacity Òran Mór Auditorium. Though Amy had thus far kept something of a low profile where the media were concerned, she took time out from her hectic schedule to give an interview with *Scotland on Sunday*. After providing its readers with a fleeting overview of Amy's life since the release of *Frank* three years earlier; particularly her blink-and-you'll-miss-it spell in rehab, and her much-publicised eating disorders, the reporter then cuts to the chase by asking Amy for her thoughts on her appearance on *The Charlotte Church Show* the previous month. But Amy is well prepared and effortlessly steals his thunder by saying she can't wait to see it herself. 'I'm just a young girl who gets fucked up sometimes,' she said candidly. 'Sometimes my head is screwed on tighter than bolts, but a lot of the time I do mess up and lose the plot like everyone does. But because I'm so defensive and sensitive I lash out a lot. I'm not a nice drunk.' When pressed to elaborate on her 'wave hello, say goodbye' rehab visit Amy responded, 'I really think if you have problems and you can't sort them out yourself you're in trouble anyway. I also got sent to food rehab, and that was exactly the same as the alcohol one. I walked in and was like, "I don't need this," and walked straight back out. I had to tell myself, "Amy, you're not the queen of the world and you don't know everything."'

*Amy poses for photographers at the Q Awards, held at London's Grosvenor House Hotel in October 2006 – the same month* Back to Black *was released.*

*Amy and one-time boyfriend Alex Jones-Donelly in February 2007 (left), and (right) with her friend, supermodel Kate Moss at New York's Gramercy Park Hotel, May 2007.*

She also gave the first hint that although she and Jones-Donelly were still together (sharing a house in Muswell Hill), all was not wine and sunshine in her love-life. 'Our relationship has become very domesticated and there's no romance anymore, no fireworks.' Realising she may have said more than she perhaps should have, she added 'But I'll make it work with him because I love him.'

The *Scotsman* was at the Òran Mór show later that evening and said of Amy's performance: 'As her new album attests, she is now Back to Black, this time hitching her wicked lyrics to an infinitely more appealing old-school soul backing.' Òran Mór translates from Gaelic as 'big song', and as such the Sistine Chapel-esque venue was perhaps the perfect setting for Amy to perform her new material. It certainly offered better acoustics than the Cottier Hall, where she'd played on her previous visit to Glasgow, and on letting herself go on some of the more vibrant numbers, it's a wonder she didn't bring the auditorium's stained-glass canopy down about the audience's heads.

The next stop on the tour was at Koko in Camden Town, which, of course, was practically on Amy's doorstep. Her new press pals from the *NME*, who were there to review what was a homecoming of sorts, said of Amy: 'She's like a wide-girl Queen Mum, sipping chardonnay on a heart-warming cockney meet and greet during the blitz, except the only bombs dropping in this venue tonight are soul-packed musical ones. Oh, and the Queen Mum never looked like a cross between Ronnie Spector and an award-winning tattooed lady from Coney Island.' It seemed as though Amy's tattoos – which numbered eleven at this point – were now receiving as much press coverage as her talents. Her most recent inking was in homage to her nan, Cynthie, who'd passed away earlier in the year, while her first – a cheeky Betty Boop on her shoulder-blade – was done when she was just fifteen. 'When my parents found out about it [the BB tattoo], they pretty much realised that I would do whatever I wanted, and that was it, really,' she subsequently told *Rolling Stone*.

♪♪♪

On taking to the stage at the Birmingham Academy two nights later, dressed in a skimpy dress and with her beehive sculpted to perfection, Amy borrowed a lipstick from a female member of the audience and asked the crowd to excuse her a moment while she put on her 'blow-job lips'. And thus the scene was well and truly set. After applying her make-up she ambled about the stage in her hooker's heels, croaking inaudibly. The audience suspected that Amy had been tucking into the rider backstage and began to fear the worst. But it seemed the only liquid Amy has been imbibing of late was Day Nurse, as she was suffering from a heavy cold. As a result, her voice was huskier than normal, but she was still determined to give heart and soul. Unfortunately, though keeping her mentally alert, the Day Nurse couldn't alleviate her throat and being the professional she was, she felt obliged to apologise whenever she failed to reach the required notes. Thankfully, however, the audience were sympathetic to her plight, and even on an off night she was worth the admission price. Despite her obvious discomfort, she still found time to joke that if she ruined her voice, then Katie Melua could always step in for her.

The previous evening, BBC Two screened Amy's appearance on its popular pop quiz show *Never Mind the Buzzcocks*. (She had, of course, appeared on the now-legendary show back in March 2004, when Mark Lamarr had held sway over the proceedings.) On that night's show she was part of Bill Bailey's team alongside Irish stand-up comedian Andrew Maxwell, going up against the show's other resident captain, Phil Jupitus, and his team of TV newsreader Penny Smith, and Alex Pennie from Welsh rockers the Automatic.

*Never Mind the Buzzcocks* is known for its dry, satirical humour, and those guests with a chequered past can expect to have their errant behaviour brought into play at some point during the show. But rather than sit there waiting to be ambushed Amy put herself in the line of fire by asking the show's incumbent host, comedian and TV presenter Simon Amstell, for a drink. With *The Charlotte Church Show* fiasco still relatively fresh in people's minds, the request was obviously meant tongue-in-cheek. Amstell, who'd acted as one of the guest hosts following Lamarr's departure before being appointed as permanent host at the beginning of the current series, first refused her request and then made a quip about her already being 'a bit tipsy'. He then got further laughs by enquiring if he and everyone else on the two teams should sit around while Amy drank herself to death, and asking her if she was aspiring to be another Pete Doherty. Amy was happy to play along and informed Amstell that she was due to meet up with Doherty in the near future to discuss their doing a duet together. Amstell warned her off from meeting the Babyshambles star, and – glancing into the camera – suggested she should instead meet up with her old Brit School pal, Katie Melua, to which Amy replied, 'I'd rather have cat Aids, thank you.'

Later on, Amstell, himself Jewish, thanked Amy for coming onto the show as part of the BBC's new remit was to have 'more Jews, less carbon emissions'. To keep the religious banter going, when it came to the round where the individual team members have to remember the next line to a well-known song, Amstell playfully asked Amy to come up with the next line to the traditional Hebrew folk song that is a staple of Jewish weddings and Bar/Bat Mitzvahs, 'Hava Nagila'. One can only imagine her family's shame when Amy couldn't think of the corresponding line, and it was left to the host – in heavily accented Hebrew – to supply the answer of 'venismechah'.

Things got a little edgy when Amy was seen to spit on the floor and Amstell playfully said, 'You come here, full of crack, spitting all over things,' to which Amy responded, 'Let it die, please.' But Amstell sensed match point in the verbal tennis and retorted in a deadpan tone, 'The addiction, I'd like to die. I want you back. This isn't even a pop quiz anymore, it's an intervention, Amy.'

♪ ♪ ♪

Amy's cold was no better when she appeared at the Manchester Academy 2 the night after her Birmingham gig, and it was undoubtedly the disappointment of having to give below par performances that led to her frustrations boiling over the next night in Norwich. Having completed her set at the Waterfront, Amy was apparently unwinding in the post-show Meltdown Disco when she took exception to a comment made by what the *Norwich Evening News* described 'a young male reveller'. Though the Waterfront is regulated by the UEA (Union of East Anglia) Student Union, the venue is open to non-students. Whether the offending comment was aimed at Amy's performance on the night or at Amy personally, the paper neglected to say. But whatever was said was enough to push Amy's buttons to the point where the club's diplomatic doormen were forced to ask her to leave. This could be the incident which she related to the *Times* that same month. 'Apparently, the other night at a gig, some girl came up to me afterwards and she goes, "Hello," and gave me a kiss on the cheek, and as she went away she goes to my boyfriend, "God, she's fucked isn't she," and I just saw red and smacked her. I don't remember this at all. Then I took my boyfriend home and started beating him up. I have a really good time some nights, but then I push it over the edge and ruin my boyfriend's night. I'm an ugly dickhead drunk, I really am.'

From Norwich, the tour proceeded to the Cambridge Junction on 20 November, and then to Bristol for the penultimate show at the Carling Academy. Three days later, Amy returned to London to appear at the Little Noise Sessions, Acoustic at the Union season at the Union Chapel in Islington, alongside her fellow singer-songwriter Mika, and multi-instrumentalist Natasha Khan, who goes under the stage name Bat for Lashes. The season, which is held annually every November and hosted by Radio One's Jo Whiley, is a fundraiser with the proceeds from ticket sales going to the learning disability charity, Mencap.

♪ ♪ ♪

Whilst on a whistle-stop tour of the UK in early December 2006 to promote *Back to Black*, Amy headed over to Belfast, where she gave interviews and performed a couple of songs at both Radio Ulster and U105. When reminiscing about Amy's visit to Radio Ulster for the *Belfast Telegraph*, the station's presenter Ralph McLean recalled, 'There was a lot of hype around her then. Because of *Back to Black*, she had come to the fore and was well on her way to being a superstar. I remember thinking her quite petulant and narky, especially with her poor guitarist. To be honest, she acted a bit like a spoilt child and I thought she was one of those stars who wouldn't quite live up

> **'I have a really good time some nights, but then I push it over the edge and ruin my boyfriend's night. I'm an ugly dickhead drunk, I really am.'** – Amy Winehouse

to the buzz around her. But when she pulled up a seat, nodded at the guitarist and began to sing "Love Is a Losing Game", I was completely blown away. She was an amazing talent. She just sat there, with her hands in the pockets of her leather jacket, chewing gum the whole time, but singing effortlessly.'

After lamenting how sad it was that more wasn't done to help get Amy back on track, like so many others before and after her, McCall remembered how Amy came alive whilst talking about music. 'She completely lit up when she was talking about music. She loved all the old sixties girl groups and really knew her stuff. She was a massive fan of the Specials and when I told her I was too, she was delighted. She could have talked forever about music.'

U105 presenter Maurice Jay was equally enamoured. 'She came into the studio, grabbed a seat and pulled up a mike. I asked her if she needed anything else, but she told me not to fuss, that she was fine, and that was that. She started singing and this incredible soulful voice came out. She sang with such raw emotion, the talent just oozed out of her. When she started talking about *Back to Black*, there was a real brightness in her eyes. I touched on her personal life and she said it had been a hard struggle, but she was reluctant to talk about it. All she wanted to talk about was her music.'

As Amy was also scheduled to perform at Dublin's Ambassador Theatre on the tour, she gave an in-depth interview to the *Irish Times* in which she candidly discussed both her professional and private life. As a means of establishing a rapport, she was asked to say what she specifically liked about each of the girl-groups that had proved a major inspiration for the songs on *Back to Black*. The Shangri-Las' prime attributes were being very dramatic and atmospheric; the Ronettes were very stylish; while the Shirelles had coolness and attitude, and the vulnerability to match. 'I loved those heartbreak songs they used to do, especially the way the girls sounded so heavenly,' she said. 'Yet they were also singing about the kind of heartbreak you would find at the bottom of a bottle of whisky. They know all about sorrow.'

> **'I loved those heartbreak songs they used to do, especially the way the girls sounded so heavenly. Yet they were also singing about the kind of heartbreak you would find at the bottom of a bottle of whisky. They know all about sorrow.'** – Amy Winehouse

When asked about the differences between recording the new album and *Frank*, Amy readily admitted that she hadn't been allowed as much control over her debut album's sound as she would have liked. 'When you have a producer with you who is far more experienced, you do tend to become a bit, "Yeah, that's cool," in the studio and go with the flow. And when you're smoking weed, you just don't care about anything except who has the next joint.' Her frustration, however, wasn't solely reserved for the recording process. 'It was my first album and I don't think the label had a clue what to do with it either, so it was a learning curve for them as well.'

It seems paradoxical that Amy would chose to casually shrug off Island's apparent failings in regard to the debut album – especially in light of her vociferous criticisms of the label in the wake of *Frank*'s release. For while she herself was undoubtedly on a learning curve at the time, Island Records, founded in 1959, had certainly been around the block enough times to know how best to market a debut album.

When Amy mentioned that she smoked weed whilst recording *Frank*, the interview neatly segued into her personal life. 'I don't smoke weed anymore so I'm not so defensive as I was back then,' she was quick to point out. 'I'm not as insecure as I was either. I go to the gym, I run loads and I'm much healthier than I was.' And yes, although she'd given up weed, and was jogging and gyming on a daily basis, she readily confessed to still enjoying a drink. 'I do drink a lot and I'm a bad drunk, a very violent drunk. It's only since I started going out with my boyfriend Alex that I have realised what a horrible drunk I am. My ex-boyfriend [Blake] would be saying things like, "Stop doing that, you're an idiot," and rowing with me when I was drunk, which just made me worse. With Alex, he will bring it up the following day when I've sobered up. It really embarrasses me to hear I've punched him in the face six times.

*Amy and singer-songwriter Pete Doherty in May 2008 (left), and (right) Amy watching Doherty's reformed band the Libertines perform at the Forum in London, August 2010.*

Of course, it does make me want to cut down on the booze. I really do try not to drink, but I'm a very self-destructive person.'

One might have thought that Amy being so candid about her drink problems in public, and her apparent lack of concern about the tightrope she was walking with a blindfold of her own choosing, would have registered on somebody's radar. And yet no one, be it family, friends, or management, thought to intervene – at least not at this stage – even though the time for tentatively suggesting that Amy seek professional guidance had evidently long since passed. What was needed now was some tough love. Those closest to her should have dragged her – kicking and screaming, if necessary – to the nearest rehab centre with Mitch Winehouse riding shotgun.

That same week, the *NME* – expanding on Amy's comments about her possibly recording a duet with Pete Doherty during her recent appearance on *Never Mind the Buzzcocks* – reported that Doherty had approached Amy with a view to the two of them cutting a Billie Holiday track together, and that Amy hadn't been overly keen on the idea as she'd seemingly been hoping that they could write a new song together. The *NME* then quoted Amy as telling BBC Radio Six, 'I was like, "No, let's write something together." I like writing songs, he's an amazing songwriter and I'd love to say that I wrote a song with Pete Doherty.'

One duet that did go ahead, however, was Amy's aforementioned performance with Paul Weller on Jools Holland's fourteenth annual end-of-year *Hootenanny*. The modfather and the soul-sister sang Marvin Gaye's 1966 Motown classic 'I Heard It Through the Grapevine', before Amy performed Toots and the Maytals' 'Monkey Man', which was something of a staple of her live set. She also joined Jools and his Rhythm and Blues Orchestra, Paul Weller, Dave McCabe, Seasick Steve, Sam Browne, Marc Almond, and some of the studio guests, for a version of Bob Dylan's folk song 'Quinn the Eskimo', which had given Manfred Mann a worldwide hit in 1968 when retitled 'Mighty Quinn'.

Lily Allen also happened to be one of Jools's guests that night. And as Amy stood watching Big Ben chiming in the New Year on the studio screen, she might have inwardly cringed at the memories of her pitiful appearance on *The Charlotte Church Show*, her uncalled for outburst towards Bono at the *Q* Awards, or her tipsy exchange with Simon Amstell on *Never Mind the Buzzcocks*. But as far as her music was concerned, 2006 had been a good year for her. *Back to Black* was sitting pretty at number 2 in the UK album chart, 'Rehab' had given her her first UK Top Ten single, and Island Universal were set to release the album in the US. All she needed to do was keep her act together in terms of her drinking, and the living would indeed be easy.

♪ ♪ ♪

On Monday, 8 January 2007, Island released 'You Know I'm No Good' as the second single from *Back to Black*. In what was becoming something of a norm, the single was again released in various formats. The UK version was released as two separate CDs, one featuring a live version of the Teddy Bears' 1958 hit 'To Know Him Is to Love Him', while the second disc featured a studio version of 'Monkey Man', as well as a 'Skeewiff mix' of the title track. With the US release date for *Back to Black* set for 13 March, another version featured a remix of the title track by Wu-Tang Clan's Ghostface Killa, with whom Mark Ronson had worked on his debut solo album *Here Comes the Fuzz*. Once again the artwork for the UK releases was in keeping with the material enclosed. One was a headshot of Amy in a suitably contemplative pose, reclining in a bathtub, while the other was of her striking an equally pensive pose whilst sat on a garden wall wearing a summer dress

Somewhat surprisingly, given that the parent album was still nestled at number 2 behind Take That's *Beautiful World* on the UK chart, the single peaked at a disappointing number 18 on the singles chart. Yet conversely, on a brighter note that same week saw 'Rehab' climb back up to number 20.

The day following the single's release Amy went some way to confirming that she was no good by putting in a shambolic performance at the GAY club night at the now demolished London Astoria at the top of Charing Cross Road. According to those present Amy tottered out onstage, struggled through one number and then fled

*Amy and her friend Kelly Osbourne share a joke on the red carpet at the* Elle *Style Awards, February 2007.*

backstage. The bemused promoter hurried out onstage to say that Amy was throwing up backstage and to bear with her. Whether this was true or merely an attempt to assuage the angry crowd mattered not, because Amy had left the building. The *Sun* subsequently reported: 'She [Amy] fled after just one song and I hear it was Kelly Osbourne's fault as the pair had been out boozing all day.'

'I'm surprised they let me in,' Amy told the *Observer* later that same month. 'I thought there would be crowds of angry homosexuals at the door, waiting to batter me! I know I look as though I can handle myself, but . . . !' And though jet-lag had undoubtedly played its part, the *Sun*'s finger-pointing accusation that Ozzy and Sharon's wayward daughter Kelly had led Amy astray was inadvertently vindicated by Amy herself. Whilst speaking to the Canadian publication *Chart Attack* a couple of months after the event, Amy said, 'I had to get off a plane, go and have a laugh with my friend [Osbourne], be silly, have a drink and then go do that show. And obviously I couldn't.'

While the UK press were again sharpening their poisoned quills, Amy flew out to New York as part of a promotional visit to the Big Apple to prepare for the album's

impending stateside release. Whilst there, she made her US live debut by performing to a sold-out crowd at Joe's Pub in Lower Manhattan on Tuesday 16 January. Indeed, such was the clamour for tickets that a second show was added for later that same night at 11:00pm. Although the venue's name – with its British 'pub' connotations – immediately conjures up images of a dingy theme bar serving stale pies and lukewarm beer to English tourists taking a break from seeing the sights, Joe's Public Theatre is actually a nightclub renowned for staging live music. Since opening its doors in October 1998, the club has become one of New York's leading live showcase venues, catering to an eclectic mix of musical genres.

With friends and celebrity guests including Mark Ronson, Jay Z, and Mos Def watching on, Amy took to the illuminated compact stage with the Dap-Kings, sporting her perfectly coiffed skyscraper beehive and a tiny bum-hugging dress that proved all the more eye-popping as to the stage was elevated. 'Anyone here from Universal? Get me more gigs,' she shouted out to no one in particular while taking measured sips from her amaretto sour and coquettishly toying with her hemline. 'Just wheel me onstage.'

> **'I had to get off a plane, go and have a laugh with my friend [Kelly Osbourne], be silly, have a drink and then go do that show. And obviously I couldn't.'** – Amy Winehouse

'It took about twenty seconds to get hooked,' writer Jason Newman – who was already aware of Amy, having been given a CDR of the *Back to Black* demo recordings – recalled recently for an MTV Amy Winehouse retrospective. 'Winehouse's words gave no quarter. She was the girl who could go shot for shot with you and win, throw a glass at somebody for provoking her and then take you record shopping with a smile on her face. Her lyrics, both on 2003's aptly named *Frank* and *Back to Black*, enraged, provoked and cracked up. It wasn't just the odd turn of phrase that her male US counterparts often utilised, but entire themes and references – missing a Slick Rick concert ('Me and Mr Jones'), drunkenly cheating on her boyfriend with a similar-looking guy – previously unheard in soul or jazz music. Most artists begged for your love. Winehouse couldn't care less. And we loved her more for it.'

And Joe's Pub's resident artist Michael Arthur later wrote on his blog: 'Everybody [was there that night]. Seriously, from what I understand, if you're in the music biz or you write about the music biz or you date someone who writes about the music biz, chances are you either had a seat or were trying to get a seat for these two shows.'

New York's press were also in attendance, and proved equally in awe. The *Village Voice* described her entrance thus: 'Backed by a taut ten-piece band, she hit the tiny stage like a tatted-up Ronette from hell, complete with thick back eyeliner, fabulously

*Blues and soul: Amy gets misty-eyed during her performance at Joe's Pub in New York on 16 January 2007 – her live debut in the US.*

ratted bouffant weave, and a skin-tight, strapless cocktail dress,' while *Spin* magazine likened Amy to a 'quintessential Bond Girl from the Sean Connery era'.

*Entertainment Weekly* opined: 'In the UK, Amy is a pop star and tabloid regular due to her outrageous behaviour, reported eating disorders, and performances where she appears to be very, very drunk. The bold-faced rappers didn't just come for spectacle, however. Sure, Winehouse keeps gossip columnists busy, but her New York coming-out proved she's much more than mere shtick.'

While she was in New York Amy gave an interview to the *Washington Post* in which she explained how certain issues and aspects of her personal life such as her alleged bulimia, anorexia, and bipolar disorder, were being totally blown out of proportion by the media. But she certainly didn't go out of her way to disarm her American fans' fears for her health, as the article ended with the reporter noting: 'She's shy and she's shaking. She stutters as she talks and searches for words, her eyes welling with tears. Her left arm is abraded and raw. Something caused the injury, but she isn't sure what. "I got drunk and I don't remember."'

A month or so later, whilst attending the *Elle* Style Awards with her new Budweiser buddy Kelly Osbourne, where she picked up the award for 'Best British Music Act', Amy admitted the not quite healed cuts and abrasions on her arms were from her having taken a drunken tumble whilst in New York, and not from self-harming as reported in the UK press.

The UK media's sole representative at the Joe's Pub show was the *Daily Mail*, which informed its readers back home: 'Despite showing some nerves, Amy won over the crowd, which included rappers Jay-Z and Mos Def, with her jazz-infused vocals perfectly backed by her tight funk band. It seems that reports that Ms Winehouse, who has been nominated for two Brit Awards, is in dire need of rehab after being forced to quit a show after one song due to feeling "tired and emotional", judged by this brilliant performance, are premature.' Had the audiences that night been aware of what had occurred in London recently, they'd have been equally dismissive of the reports, because as the *Washington Post* succinctly put it the following day: 'Folks are clapping and woo-hooing, and proclaiming her brilliant.'

It seemed the *Daily Mail* had something of a scoop in relating Amy's nominations for the two Brit awards, as – owing to the five-hour time difference between London and New York – it wasn't until the following morning that the news from home reached Amy herself. The awards in question were for British Female Solo Artist, in which she would be up against Lilly Allen, Corinne Bailey Rae, Jamelia, and Nerina Pallot; and in the Mastercard British Album category, in which she faced competition from Snow Patrol, Muse, Arctic Monkeys, and Lily Allen.

♪ ♪ ♪

*An immaculately made-up Amy attends the*
Elle *Style Awards in London, February 2007.*

Having wowed New York, Amy returned to London for a wash and a brush-up before embarking on her first European dates. The mini-European jaunt saw her take in shows at Berlin's Kalkscheune on 24 January, and then at the Rockerfeller in Oslo two days later. Amy then returned to London for a show at the Shepherd's Bush Empire, before flying out to Amsterdam to play the city's legendary Club Paradiso. On her return to London she set about preparing for the opening date of the UK leg of her forthcoming *Back to Black* tour, at the Cambridge Corn Exchange on Saturday 17 February.

She took time out from rehearsals to attend the Brit Awards ceremony, staged at the Earl's Court Exhibition Centre, where aside from performing 'Rehab' live on the night, she picked up the award for Best British Female Artist. Yet, despite *Back to Black* having sold in excess of 500,000 in the UK, knocking Take That off their lofty perch to claim the top spot on the UK album chart, Amy had to watch host Russell Brand hand the best album award to the Arctic Monkeys for their debut album, *Whatever People Say I Am, That's What I'm Not.*

> 'In the long term I have more family plans. I've got to a point where I've made an album which I'm proud of. Now I need to follow that up, but to have kids as well. Then go to Vegas, open my own casino and perform there every night!' – Amy Winehouse

Of course, with her picking up the Brit for Best British Female Artist, and her new album residing at number 1 on the chart, it was only to be expected that the media would be interested in her thoughts on her contemporaries. Later that month she would play down the Brit Awards win. 'That's cool. Whatever. I don't care about that,' she told *Music OMH*. 'I'm not the kind of person that would ever have gone if I wasn't nominated.'

When asked about her long-term plans Amy retorted, 'In the long term I have more family plans. I've got to a point where I've made an album which I'm proud of. Now I need to follow that up, but to have kids as well. Then go to Vegas, open my own casino and perform there every night!' She'd said something similar to the *Guardian* back in 2004, about going to Vegas when she was in her sixties – 'when I can't grasp reality any more' – to sing standards. And one cannot help but conjure up images of a slightly tipsy, middle-aged Amy, with her make-up smudged and her beehive wig askew, a glass in one hand, while the other grips the microphone stand that serves as her anchor, entertaining the gamblers with Dean Martin staples such as 'Ain't That a Kick in the Head', 'That's Amore', and 'Little Ole Wine Drinker Me'.

♪ ♪ ♪

*Lady in red: Amy during rehearsals for the 2007 Brit Awards.*

The *Independent* was on hand to witness Amy's first post-Brits victory outing, but surprisingly, given the paper's staunch support, the review was less than complimentary. 'Ever since her sozzled performance on *The Charlotte Church Show*, Winehouse has become notorious for liking a drink. Though this threatens to define her in the media, it's likely that it just makes her a normal young girl. But this gig at the Cambridge Corn Exchange, her first since her Brit award, does her few favours, cursed as it is with aircraft-hangar acoustics and a boozy crowd. Winehouse, with her black cocktail dress and tottering beehive, seems dressed for a more sophisticated affair. The disjunction between the kind of venue success brings and the intimate nature of what she actually does cripples the show.'

Though appreciative of Amy's Aretha-esque ability to stitch the notes together to mean more than the lyrics, and of her backing band's smorgasbord of musical genres, ranging from delightful acoustic jazz guitar (assumingly borrowed from her dad's late-fifties Sinatra records, when Ol' Blues Eyes was working with renowned arranger Nelson Riddle and released some of the most heart-wrenching albums ever recorded), slinky Bossa nova shuffles, seventies soul-funk, ska, and Cuban brass that was more 'Clash than Cullum', the critique ends with a hint of advisory caution. 'Her success may be dragging Amy Winehouse into inappropriate places, but that's the price of making pop music this good.'

The *Independent* is right on the money here, because Amy's growing popularity was indeed forcing her into inappropriate settings for her music. The natural order in rock'n'roll is that a band or artist sets out playing anywhere that will have them to get their name known, secure a recording contract, sell more and more records, play bigger and bigger venues, until reaching the apex of sell-out arena shows and a sea of raised arms punching the air in tandem with the chorus. Amy's dilemma was that while she could effortlessly sell out the Shepherd's Bush Empire, or the O2 Arena, sultry soul stirrings such as hers were best suited to more intimate and sedate surroundings. After all, Amy's songs of heartbreak and despair were autobiographical, and baring one's soul is usually done in whispers in a darkened corner, not hollered across a crowded room.

Following on from Cambridge, the tour proceeded to Southampton for a show at the Guildhall on the 18 February, and then a brief return to the capital for a show at the Astoria, where Amy made amends by playing a full set. From there it continued to the more familiar stomping grounds of Birmingham 02 Academy, Liverpool 02 Academy, and then Manchester 02 Academy on 25 February, and the following day saw Amy make another return to Newcastle's Northumbria University. As with her previous tours, Amy also made a return to Glasgow, but due to her public's demand this time it was at the larger Glasgow Academy. And the *Glasgow Herald* was of a similar opinion to the *Independent* when it came to the choice of venue. 'Incredible though it is, her voice is only part of what makes Winehouse such a unique talent. In this environment, however, the majority of her cheeky, barbed lyrics are lost.'

Having played to an ecstatic sell-out crowd at Belfast's Ulster Hall, Amy then crossed the border for the second Irish date at Dublin's Ambassador Theatre. Four years earlier she'd been playing the Dublin Castle pub in Camden, and now here she was playing a 1,200-capacity venue in the Irish capital itself. After opening its review with an amusing aside about Amy arriving onstage sporting 'a wonderfully ornate hairstyle that would make Marge Simpson's 'do look like a short back-and-sides,' the *Irish Times* also felt that at times Amy's lack of stage presence made what was emanating from the stage feel like 'background music at a large social event'. And while opining that Amy still had some way to go, the writer recognised that she undoubtedly had what it took to achieve greatness as a live performer.

> **'I'm not ruling out rehab. Amy needs a break. They don't send you to rehab just because you've broken up with someone. She's an emotional girl.'** – Mitch Winehouse

Having conquered Ireland, it was back over to the mainland for shows in Sheffield, Nottingham, and Cardiff, and then London for what was intended as a triumphant return to the capital, with two sell-out shows at the Shepherd's Bush Empire. However, the two London finale shows ended up being postponed until the end of May.

One explanation for the enforced cancellations – which was subsequently supported by photos of a grinning, gap-toothed Amy that appeared in the media – was that Amy's singing voice had been affected after she inadvertently lost a tooth when biting down on an ice cube. The more likely reason, however, was Amy's state of mind following her split with Alex Jones-Donelly. The relationship had been suffering for some time because of Amy's gruelling workload, and it appeared Alex had finally grown tired of having to book appointments through Amy's PA to see her. When rumours about Amy seeking medical help started doing the rounds in the wake of the London cancellations, Mitch Winehouse told the *Sunday Mirror*, 'I'm not ruling out rehab. Amy needs a break. They don't send you to rehab just because you've broken up with someone. She's an emotional girl. Her schedule has caused problems with Alex. I don't know if that's the reason for the break-up, but wouldn't you want to see your boyfriend now and again?'

# 8. I Know
# He's No Good

'I really thought I was on the way out. My husband Blake saved my life. Often I don't know what I do, then the next day the memory returns. And then I am engulfed in shame.'

To further whet America's appetite, on the day that *Back to Black* went on general release in the US, Amy returned to New York for the opening show of a four-date mini-tour at the city's Bowery Ballroom. She also made her high-profile American TV debut with an appearance on the *Late Show with David Letterman*, on which she performed 'Rehab'. Following on from there, she headed down to Texas to perform at the Universal Republic Showcase at the South by Southwest Festival four days later, before flying out to the West Coast for two shows in Los Angeles. The first of these was on 19 March at the Roxy Theatre on LA's legendary Sunset Strip, where the VIP guest-list boasted celebrities such as Bruce Willis, Courtney Love and Fabrizio Moretti, the Brazilian-born drummer from the Strokes. But the second date at Spaceland, in the trendy upmarket Silverlake district, was cancelled at the eleventh hour owing to – if the *NME* is to be believed – Amy's doubts about the venue's postage stamp-sized stage being able to accommodate her full band.

By the time Amy boarded a plane at LAX, *Back to Black* had shifted over 50,000 copies and slammed onto the *Billboard* 200 at number 7, making it the highest debut entry for an album by a British female solo artist in *Billboard*'s sixty-one-year history. (The accolade would prove short-lived when Joss Stone went one better the following week.) In their reviews, the American critics were as complimentary as their English cousins. Indeed, such was the buzz surrounding the album that *Metacritic*, which assigns normalised ratings from zero to one hundred based on reviews from mainstream critics, gave the album an average score of eighty-one based on twenty-six reviews, which indicated 'universal acclaim', no less. The reviews were universally

*Red-carpet romance: Amy and Blake arrive at the MTV Movie Awards in June 2007.*

appreciative of the album's modern reimagining of Motown-era R&B and soul. *Allmusic*'s John Bush was particularly enthusiastic about Amy's musical transition and gave the album five stars, gushing, 'Although *Back to Black* does see her [Amy] deserting jazz and wholly embracing contemporary R&B, all the best parts of her musical character emerge intact, and actually, are all the better for the transformation from jazz vocalist to soul siren.'

Jake Henneman at *Crawdaddy!* cited the album's musical direction as 'sensuous, neo-soul and R&B', while *Entertainment Weekly* critic Chris Willman declared the album to be 'one of the great breakthrough CDs of our time', and ended by opining: 'In the end, the singer's real-life heartache [. . .] proves what's obvious from the grooves: when this lady sings about love, she means every word.'

♪ ♪ ♪

Another thirteen-date US jaunt was scheduled for the end of April, but before then Amy performed at the third annual Camden Crawl, alongside the likes of Travis, Kate Nash, Adele, Babyshambles, and Black Rebel Motorcycle Club.

Given that Camden was Amy's home, and the place where she'd first started out, playing the Crawl with her album selling strong on both sides of the Atlantic must have seemed like a fairytale come true. But as with all the classic fairytales, this one had a villain lurking in the mist. Just three days before Amy was due to fly out to America, and while the gossip columns were still chuckling over Alex Jones-Donelly having sold his story to the *News of the World* (which published his sordid sex-romp tale under the headline: 'Bondage Crazed Amy Just Can't Beehive in Bed'), the *Sunday Mirror* broke the news that Amy was not only back with Blake Fielder-Civil, but that the couple were actually engaged. What's more, it was rumoured that Blake had agreed to convert to Judaism so they might have a Jewish wedding sometime during the summer. And the following day, the *Sun* announced that Blake had popped the question whilst the couple were holed away in Amy's flat, and that after keeping her lover hanging on tenterhooks for twenty-four hours, Amy had said yes. Those same gossip columnists – and the vast majority of Amy's fans – were quick to brand Blake a money-grabber, while others might have argued that, seeing as he'd inadvertently been the inspiration for the majority of the songs on the hit album, he was merely collecting his dues. Either way, Camden's unofficial queen was reunited with her king.

Regardless of any objections Raye Cosbert or anyone at Island may have had, Amy insisted that her fiancé accompany her to California for the tour's opening date at San Francisco's Popscene, where she appeared alongside the Klaxons on Thursday 26 April. The following night Amy played the opening night of the ninth annual Coachella Valley Music and Arts Festival, staged within the Empire Polo Grounds in Indio. Such was the festival's popularity that this year it had been extended to three days, and though Amy appeared on an impressive bill that included rock heavyweights

*LA woman: Amy onstage at the Roxy in Los Angeles in March 2007 (left) and (right) Amy and Blake share a kiss on the streets of New York, August 2007.*

such as the Red Hot Chili Peppers, Rage Against the Machine, Kings of Leon, and the Kaiser Chiefs, Indio lies within the California Desert and performing in 100-degree heat left her drained.

On Monday 30 April, the same day Amy was set to appear at the Fox Theatre in Boulder, Colorado, Island Records – no doubt hoping to further cash in on Amy's popularity – released 'Back to Black' as the third single from the album in the UK. The cover shot was taken from the same shoot as the one used for 'Rehab' remix single, yet despite being backed with versions of the Specials' 'Hey Little Rich Girl', and the Zutons' 'Valerie' – neither of which was available elsewhere – the single stalled at number 25 on the chart.

After playing shows in Minneapolis, Chicago, Philadelphia, and Boston, Amy arrived back in the Big Apple for two shows at the Highline Ballroom commencing on 8 May. 'I love America, it's a much more permissive place,' she'd told the *Guardian* back in 2004. 'Here in England, everyone's a pop star, innit, whereas in America they believe in the term artist.' Having wrapped up the latest US tour with two shows at the Mod Club in Toronto, Canada, Amy and Blake then flew down to Miami where – according to the mounting media speculation now surrounding the couple's every move – they would be tying the knot. Though Amy usually remained tight-lipped whenever she and Blake were out soaking up the Florida sunshine, she told *Entertainment Weekly*: 'We've been back together about a month. But we've been seeing a lot of each other for quite a few months. We are best friends.' This tantalising titbit about possible clandestine liaisons having occurred prior to her appearance at the Camden Crawl only served to fuel the rumours that something was set to happen. And on Friday 18 May, Amy and Blake stood before God and the officiant at the Miami-Dade County Marriage Licence Bureau to be pronounced man and wife. Though money was an issue Amy no longer needed to worry about, the cost of the marriage license, and the ensuing wedding breakfast of hamburgers and fries, came to just £60. 'We're not planning a honeymoon,' Amy told the *Daily Mail*. 'Every day is a honeymoon. I've married the best man in the world.'

> **'We're not planning a honeymoon. Every day is a honeymoon. I've married the best man in the world.'** – Amy Winehouse

The following day, the *Daily Mail* reported that Amy and Blake had announced they were to have a second wedding on their return to London so that their families could participate. 'I'm so glad I got married to Blake. We've been in love for such a long time but we didn't realise it until lately,' Amy told the paper. She then played down reports about Blake supposedly converting to Judaism. 'People have been talking about me having a Jewish wedding, but I'm not interested in that, that's bullshit. We are just going to have a nice family party to celebrate in December.' When the paper enquired as to what her parents' reactions were on reading about their daughter's wedding in the newspapers, Amy said: 'My dad was alright about it really, it was more my mum that wasn't. I would have loved my family to have been there but it was something just for us.'

Amy's comment about waiting until December before throwing the second wedding party might have sounded strange given that it was only May, but her schedule was such that she barely had time to pick out the 'his and hers' towels before returning to the glare of the public spotlight at the fifty-second Ivor Novello Awards, once again staged at the Grosvenor House Hotel on Park Lane. Amy had been nominated in the Best Contemporary Song category for 'Rehab', where she faced stiff competition from the likes of Hot Chip ('Over and Over') and Bodyrox ('Yeah Yeah'). But in a year when she could seemingly do no wrong – if only in her professional life – just as she had in 2004, Amy walked away with the prize.

*Time* magazine would subsequently list 'Rehab' as number 1 on its 'Ten Best

*His 'n' hers: Amy and Blake wear matching outfits backstage at the Isle of Wight Festival in June 2007.*

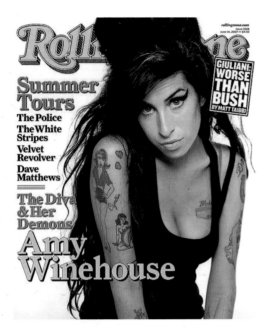

Songs of 2007'. When asked the reason why *Time* had chosen the song, the magazine's compiler, Josh Tyrangiel, responded: 'While she [Amy] is mouthy, funny, sultry, and quite possibly crazy, it's impossible not to be seduced by her originality. Combine this with production by Mark Ronson that references four decades worth of soul music without once ripping it off, and you've got the best song of 2007.'

♪ ♪ ♪

Flushed with the success of having a second Ivor on the mantelpiece, Amy flew out to Landgraaf, Holland, to appear at the Pinkpop Festival at Megaland, before returning to London to play the two rescheduled Shepherd's Bush Empire shows. 'Don't know if you heard,' the *Daily Mail* reported her as saying midway through the opening night's show, 'but I just got married to the best man in the entire world.' She then proceeded to blow kisses to Blake, who was up in the VIP balcony.

With the summer festival season getting into gear, Amy only had a couple of days respite before flying out to Germany to appear at the Rock Im Park 2007 at Zeppelinfeld, Nürnberg. A week or so later it was to Seaclose Park in Newport, and the prestigious Isle of Wight Festival, where, aside from wowing the crowd with her own set, the following night she joined event headliners the Rolling Stones onstage for a blistering version of the Temptations' 1966 soul classic 'Ain't Too Proud to Beg'.

With the Stones making their first British festival appearance in over thirty years, the festival had sold out its 60,000 ticket allocation within five days of going on sale. And within a week of hogging the centre-stage limelight with Mick and Keef, while the lady herself was in Sweden preparing for the Hultsfredsfestivalen, Amy appeared on the front cover of *Rolling Stone* magazine. Accompanied by some excellent photos, the in-depth interview – under the telling headline 'The Diva and Her Demons' – provided those of its readers as yet unfamiliar with Amy with a recap of her recent offstage escapades, such as her drinking and alleged self-harming, her verbal tennis spat with *Never Mind the Buzzcocks* host Simon Amstell, and her heckling Bono at the *Q* Awards, as well as the fact that two songs from *Back to Black* ('Rehab' and 'Love Is

*Like a rolling stone: Amy onstage with Mick Jagger during the Rolling Stones' headlining set at the Isle of Wight Festival, June 2007.*

*A glazed-eyed Amy onstage at the Glastonbury Festival in June 2007.*

a Losing Game') were being covered by rap icon Jay-Z and purple pop pixie Prince respectively. Given the interview's emphasis on Amy's volatile personality rather than her music, it's fair to say that many of those perusing the article might've been left pondering what was so unusual about a Limey pop star drinking excessively and publicly voicing her opinions, and whether that merited her being given the front cover, but as Mark Ronson is quoted as saying within the article, Amy was indeed bringing rock'n'roll's rebellious spirit back to pop music.

There was more good news stateside, because 'Rehab' had climbed into the Top Ten of the *Billboard* Hot 100 the week ending 14 June. Everyone at Island Universal must surely have been expecting even greater things for the record following Amy's spellbinding performance of the song at the 2007 MTV Movie Awards in New York that same week. However, when the chart was published the following week the single had only moved up a solitary place.

Following on from her appearance at the 2007 Zulu Rocks Festival in Copenhagen on Saturday 16 June, Amy arrived back in England on the summer solstice for the main event on the festival calendar: Glastonbury. Unlike her 2004 appearance, however, Amy put in a lacklustre performance, with the *Guardian* going so far as to opine, 'Though Winehouse's live voice is flawless, she bares more than a passing resemblance to a rabbit caught in the headlights. It takes a few songs to shake off the nerves, but she never quite loses the slightly traumatised expression.'

It should have been obvious to all within her immediate circle that Amy was showing serious signs of burnout. Yet instead of cancelling subsequent appearances at European festivals in Norway, Belgium and France, so that she might recharge her batteries before returning to the UK, it was her British fans who were set to miss out. Indeed, some 4,500 of those left disappointed were already gathered inside Liverpool's Aintree Pavilion in anticipation of seeing their heroine when a spokesman announced that Amy had been advised to pull the show on the orders of a local doctor who'd examined her backstage. Hopes that Amy might recover in time for her scheduled appearance at T in the Park two days later were dashed when Amy's management issued a statement citing exhaustion as a result of her non-stop touring and promotion commitments as the reason for the cancellations. Planned appearances at Dublin's Oxygen Festival and the North Sea Jazz Festival in Rotterdam were also sidelined. Though Amy would have been loath to cancel any shows, having to cancel her appearance at the jazz festival must have been particularly galling considering her old 'new jazz' nemesis Katie Melua was also appearing on the bill. On hearing about the latest cancellations, *Heat* magazine took to running a regular feature called 'Where's Wino?' while the *Sun*'s showbiz 'Bizarre' column uncharitably nicknamed her 'Amy Declinehouse'.

Though the doctors hadn't specified how long it might take for Amy to regain her strength – both physically and mentally – the proof that she'd discharged herself from the recovery room too soon came at the Eden Project at St Austell, Cornwall, on Tuesday 17 July. According to various press reports Amy appeared to be in tears while onstage, and was smacking herself around the head and in the face with the microphone in obvious frustration at forgetting the words to her songs. Those fans gathered at the front of the stage were saying that she'd repeatedly spat at them throughout the shambling performance. After the show, a spokesperson defended Amy's onstage behaviour by saying she'd simply been venting her frustrations: 'She is a bit ring-rusty after not having played for a while and was upset after making a few mistakes in the set.' With hindsight, it's now easy to see that while Amy was no doubt exhausted, late nights spent popping pills and other potions with Blake were probably as much to blame as the tour schedule.

Whatever was ailing Amy in St Austell had been banished by the following day, when she returned to Liverpool's Aintree Pavilion to play the rescheduled Summer Pops show. According to BBC Liverpool, who were there to review the proceedings, the first thing Amy did after taking to the stage was to apologise for the last-minute 'bottling-out' cancellation of a fortnight earlier, as well as thank the crowd for having her back. And it seemed the wait was worth it, as the reviewer wrote of Amy's performance: 'You couldn't help but be astounded by the sheer power of her voice, which seemed to emanate effortlessly from her tiny lungs no matter which jazzy-soul song from the latest album *Back to Black* she was performing.'

It did indeed appear as though Amy was back to her fighting best, and after putting in a solid performance at the Summer Series staged at Somerset House in central London (where she told the crowd, 'I've been here at least an hour and I haven't even collapsed'), she flew to Spain to perform at the Benicassim Festival on 22 July, before returning to London for a show at the rather more intimate iTunes festival at the ICA (Institute of Contemporary Arts) three days later. According to the *Daily Mail*'s subsequent report, Amy – backed by a nine-piece band decked out in sixties-style slick black suits, while she herself was clad in a vintage black and white dress – put in a brilliant performance which served as a timely reminder as to why she'd collected the Brit Award for Best British Female Artist earlier in the year, and was the bookies' odds-on favourite to add that year's much-coveted Mercury Music Prize to her trophy

> **'I've been here at least an hour and I haven't even collapsed.'**
> **– Amy Winehouse**

haul. Even her keeping the punters waiting some fifty minutes before arriving onstage failed to dampen the *Mail*'s ardour. 'Winehouse achieved instant forgiveness for her poor timekeeping as soon as she opened her mouth. "Tears Dry on Their Own", which made good use of the band's brass section, showed off her breathtaking voice. Live, even more so than on CD, Winehouse's voice was truly soulful.'

Following on from two shows performing with the Artic Monkeys and Supergrass at the Lancashire County Cricket Ground, Amy flew out to Baltimore to appear at the Virgin Festival alongside the Beastie Boys and the reformed Police. She then played the final day of the three-day Lollapalooza Festival in Chicago on 5 August, before returning to London in preparation for her forthcoming appearance at the Øya Festival in Norway, set to take place on 9 August. But on the eve of the festival – whilst her band were onstage running through their sound-check – news came through from London that Amy wasn't feeling very well. Those closest to her assumed that Amy was simply suffering from another bout of exhaustion. But this latest breakdown was more serious . . . far more serious.

♪ ♪ ♪

Acting on doctors' orders Amy was once again confined to bed, but in the early hours of the following morning a deeply concerned Blake – aided by one of Amy's female friends – half-carried a barely-conscious Amy into the A&E department of the

*Amy and her infamous beehive work the crowd at Lollapalooza 2007 in Chicago, Illinois.*

University College London Hospital, where she reportedly shrieked in agony before collapsing to the floor. The attendant nurses rushed Amy through to the treatment area, where the emergency team gave her an adrenaline shot to steady her erratic heartbeat, then pumped her stomach, and once she was stabilised she was admitted into the hospital.

With her performance at the Øya Festival officially cancelled, and her backing band and road crew making their way to the airport, Blake sat by Amy's bed anxiously awaiting the doctors' prognosis while Raye Cosbert met with Darcus Beese, and everyone else at Island Records involved with Amy, to discuss how best to handle the situation once the media got wind of the story – as they surely would do.

It didn't take long. Two days after Amy was admitted the *Sun*'s banner headline of Thursday 9 August proclaimed: 'Wild Pop Star Has Adrenaline Jab and Stomach Pumped: Amy in Drugs Collapse'. It was a long time since the tabloids had been gifted with such a story, and they were determined to wring every last debauched drop from the sensational tale. After regaling its readers with details of party-loving pop star Amy being dragged into A&E with her trademark beehive hair hanging lank about her shoulders, then collapsing from a huge drugs overdose and being rushed through for emergency treatment, the paper proceeded to recount how tattooed Amy, whose stick-thin frame and sallow complexion had long been worrying friends and fans alike, had previously admitted to heavy boozing, and using marijuana and cocaine.

That same day's edition of the free paper *London Lite* speculated that Amy was 'seriously considering' checking into a treatment programme after her 'suspected overdose'. The paper then quoted a 'close friend' who claimed that Amy had got a massive fright from being hospitalised, and was finally coming round to her friends and family's pleadings for her to go into rehab. 'She now realises she may need help as her lifestyle finally takes its toll.' The following day's edition announced that Amy had indeed checked herself into the world-famous Priory clinic in Roehampton.

With the genie now out in the open air, the *Sun*, having declared something of an open-season on Amy, again dedicated its front-page to Amy's plight, and under the equally lurid headline 'Amy's Three-Day Binge: Coke, Ecstasy, Horse Tranquiliser, Vodka, Whisky', went on to explain in sordid detail what it had discovered about Amy's activities following her arrival back at Heathrow from Chicago (though strangely made no mention of Amy's supposed trip to Roehampton). According to its sources, once Amy had been met at the arrivals gate by Blake, the couple had set off hand-in-hand for the Robert Inn in nearby Hounslow, where they'd guzzled down copious amounts of vodka and lager, shot some pool, and – according to one of the locals – made 'repeated visits to the toilets'. The next port of call on the alleged three-day bender was at the much closer-to-home Hawley Arms, where 'a fan' told the paper that he'd seen Amy knocking back the rock'n'roll drink of champions, Jack Daniel's, before she and Blake invited everyone back to theirs. The paper then quoted a friend of Blake's as saying, 'It was like she [Amy] had pressed the self-destruct button. She was downing coke, pills and ketamine [the horse tranquiliser alluded to in the article's headline], vodka and Jack Daniel's.'

The same 'friend' also told the paper of how Amy had picked up a pink guitar at one point, only to put it down again after a bit of desultory strumming and then burst into tears. Another who wished to remain anonymous said that Amy had already been telling everyone willing to listen that she hadn't slept for three days when she'd started convulsing. According to the second friend's story, it was at this point that 'Blake called friends'. (At least that's what they were claiming to be.) On realising that Amy wasn't coming round, it was decided they should get her to the nearest A&E unit. The *Sun* then told of how Amy's father had visited her in hospital, and that after being given the all-clear by the doctors, she was discharged and left the hospital by a rear exit.

The following day saw Amy score a hat-trick of front-page headlines with the same paper when the *Sun* declared: 'Amy Winehouse – I'm Suicidal'. After disclosing another disturbing development – that Amy had supposedly smoked heroin on the night of her overdose – the paper continued its progress report by stating that Amy – who was reported to be booked into the Four Seasons Hotel in Hook, Hampshire, since leaving hospital – was actually desperately ill. 'She [Amy] has been unable to eat and has been vomiting non-stop. She has been visited by doctors and a psychiatrist is due to see her today.' The article concluded with an unnamed Winehouse family friend saying, 'Amy has told her mum she is often suicidal and knows she will die young.'

Those fans staking out the Four Seasons Hotel in the hope of catching a glimpse of their idol were on something of a wasted errand, as it was then reported that Amy and Blake were in the US being treated for their heroin and crack-cocaine addictions. According to the *Daily Mirror*'s 'Star's Mum-In-Law Talks' headline scoop of Wednesday 15 August, following her release from hospital Amy had apparently summoned her dad and step-mum Jane, as well as her in-laws Georgette and Giles Civil, to the hotel for a family summit on 10 August, where – over Ovaltine and chocolate cake – she'd confessed to her and Blake's drug use. Forty-two-year-old Georgette told the paper, 'It's the hardest thing in the world for me to say in public that my son and his wife have a drug problem. They've admitted it.' Georgette then went to claim that Blake had had a drug problem ever since moving down to London when he was twenty.

> **'When he came off the island, Blake said, "I like being a drug addict. I like being on drugs. I have no intention of coming off drugs." At that point I thought, "We're in trouble here."'**
> **– Mitch Winehouse**

Admitting to an addiction isn't quite the same as acting on it, because – according to the *Mirror* – no sooner had the clear-the-air talks ended than Amy and Blake went and scored some heroin and smoked it in their room. The following morning, however, their nefarious nocturnal activities were uncovered when Amy's ex-flatmate Juliette Ashby, who was also staying at the hotel, found telltale charred pieces of silver foil on the bedside table. Juliette was so incensed at what she saw as her friend's betrayal that she reported her discovery to Mitch Winehouse. Mitch was said to have been furious, and blamed Blake for Amy's addictions. This in turn prompted Georgette to call an eminent Harley Street GP, who came to the Four Seasons and set about making arrangements for Amy and Blake to be booked into a treatment centre at a secret location in America.

But before these headline stories could even be used as fish and chip wrappings, contradictory clues as to Amy's and Blake's whereabouts were appearing in the following day's *Sun*, which bore the headline: 'Amy Quits Essex Rehab'. The Essex rehab centre in question was the Causeway Clinic, where – if the *Sun*'s story was correct – Amy and Blake had been admitted on the Monday, but had discharged themselves just forty-eight hours later, after Georgette's revelations had appeared in the *Daily Mirror*.

Mitch Winehouse later told the *Sun*, 'They went to Osea Island in Essex, by helicopter. The only way you can get on the island is when the tide is out. I thought, "There's no way they can get drugs in there." But Blake got a fisherman to bring them in for them. When he came off the island, Blake said, "I like being a drug addict. I like being on drugs. I have no intention of coming off drugs." At that point I thought, "We're in trouble here." Amy was saying she couldn't be doing it any more – but her husband actually wanted to continue.'

According to the paper's apparently well-informed sources, Amy and Blake had booked a helicopter to ferry them back to Camden before then heading to Harley Street, presumably to consult with the same GP Georgette had summoned to the Four Seasons. The article also mentioned that Mitch Winehouse was looking into getting a restraining order taken out against Blake, in the hope that his doing so would

> '**Look at me, I'm a mess. I'm nothing special. In fact I'm nothing at all. I don't feel good. I don't have talent. I feel flattered you'd say that, but I know it's not true. I'm useless and just keep messing up.'** – Amy Winehouse

give Amy a better chance of coming to her senses and seeking independent help for her drink and drug problems. That same evening's edition of *London Lite* ran a story saying that, on their return to Camden, Amy and Blake were seen out enjoying a drink or two in the Old Eagle pub with Georgette and Giles. To add veracity to the claim, the free paper carried a quote from Giles, saying how he and Georgette had been praying that Amy and Blake would stick to the treatment programme, and that they hadn't wanted them 'to go back into their vicious cycle'.

Later that same month, Georgette gave an interview with BBC Radio Five. Georgette told the interviewer she believed that, unless Amy and Blake sought medical help, one, if not both of them, were sure to die. Giles expressed his forthright concern that if one of them died, then the other was sure to follow. 'They're a very close couple,' he said. 'And if one dies through substance abuse, the other may commit suicide.'

And what were Island Records doing while all this was going on? Well, seeing as the tabloids had given Amy maximum exposure, they busied themselves with preparing 'Tears Dry on Their Own', backed with the previously unreleased track 'You're Wondering Now', as the fourth single release from *Back to Black*. The artwork – obviously hurried through – features a cover shot of a close-up of Amy taken from the same fifties kitsch shoot used for the 'Rehab' remix and 'Back to Black' single. One more such release and fans would have a set of matching coasters.

As with previous Amy Winehouse products, the single was released in several formats, including both seven-inch and twelve-inch vinyl, and featured different remixes of the title track. Their strategy paid unexpected dividends when the single reached a very respectable number 16 on the UK chart.

♪ ♪ ♪

On the day Amy had been due to appear at the V Festival before having to cancel this – and the forthcoming Rock en Seine Festival in Paris on 25 August – on doctors' orders, the *Sunday Mirror* carried an interview with Amy in which she candidly laid her cards on the table. 'Look at me, I'm a mess,' she said. 'I'm nothing special. In fact I'm nothing at all. I don't feel good. I don't have talent. I feel flattered you'd say that, but I know it's not true. I'm useless and just keep messing up.'

When the interviewer asked about Blake, Amy responded, 'I love him so much sometimes it hurts. I owe him everything. Without him I would be nothing, which is why it is so important we are together right now. I can't beat the drugs without him. He's my rock and as a married couple we need to go through everything together. Blake says he isn't going back to rehab – but I can if I want. But I'm not going without him. I'm lucky I've got a caring husband – I don't deserve him. I can't believe he even wants to be with me. I don't understand why. All I know is I'm the luckiest girl alive to have someone as caring as Blake.' At moments like this, low ebbs during which she labelled herself talentless and worthless and emphasised her total dependence on Blake, it seemed that the confident and provocative young woman who'd first appeared on the music scene in 2004 was gone forever.

While Amy's fans in the UK and Europe were rueing the latest cancellations, on 21 August the news broke that Amy was cancelling her entire forthcoming US tour, which consisted of prestigious theatres in major cities, as well as several high-profile outdoor festivals, the first of which was on Wednesday 12 September in Central Park, New York. Her publicist said that as Amy had been ordered to rest by her doctors, there'd been little option but to reschedule the US dates for early the following year. This was a particularly bitter pill to swallow for all concerned, as the tour had been arranged to capitalise on 'Rehab' giving Amy her first US Top Ten hit and further boost Amy's profile in the US.

A lot of hard work had gone into arranging the tour, but unlike the vast majority of corporations the world over, Island Universal were willing to put people before profit. And as *Back to Black* was still holding its own in the upper reaches of the *Billboard* 200, there was little sign of Amy's stateside popularity waning anytime soon.

Unfortunately, the UK media's ongoing fascination with Amy's offstage escapades was also showing little sign of abating, and it wasn't long before she and Blake were once again front-page news. But according to the latest dispatches from the front, it wasn't just the headlines they were hitting.

# 9. Glad to Be Unhappy

**'I've always been a little homemaker. I know I'm talented, but I wasn't put here to sing. I was put here to be a wife and a mum and to look after my family. I love what I do, but it's not where it begins and ends.'**

If it could be said that Amy and Blake's personal life resembled a circus, then the time to send in the clowns came with reports of the couple's late-night bust-up at the Sanderson Hotel on Berners Street in central London, where they were staying. According to the *Daily Mail*'s lead story of Friday 24 August, at sometime between 2:30 and 3:00am a 'badly-bleeding' Blake was seen chasing a distraught Amy out of their £500-a-night room and along the corridor to the lift. A guest who happened to be in the lift at the time told the paper, 'Amy was in floods of tears. This guy [Blake] was screaming at her. She was cowering in the corner and I thought he was going to hit her. When the lift door opened, she took off across the lobby at a real pace. He was chasing after her and was about five paces behind by the time she got to the main hotel entrance.'

Another 'eagle-eyed witness' said: 'Just after 3:00am, Amy came sprinting out and down the road. She was in a real state of panic. Blake was running after her, but couldn't catch up. Amy was so hell-bent on getting away from him that she ran into the middle of the street and flagged down a random car that happened to be full of girls.' According to other sources, the girls had dropped Amy off at Charing Cross train station, where she apparently purchased a pack of Camel Lights cigarettes at a twenty-four-hour shop. One can only imagine what these girls thought on finding Amy Winehouse standing in the middle of the road and forcing them to a halt. Hell, they'll probably be dining out on that one for some years to come.

Blake had apparently chased after the car for a while before giving up and returning to Berners Street, where he was supposed to have 'spent the next half hour

*Blake's girl: Amy performs at the 46664 Concert in Celebration of Nelson Mandela's Life, held at London's Hyde Park on 27 June 2008.*

or so wandering around in a daze with blood over his face, looking in doorways for her [Amy], shouting her name out', despite having just seen her drive away – which is in itself indicative of the state he must have been in.

He then managed to get through to Amy on his mobile, and after 'a lot of tears and shouting' Amy finally revealed her whereabouts. A short time later the quarrelling couple – with the paparazzi shadowing their every step – made their way back to the hotel walking hand-in-hand.

From what the paper could ascertain from the other guests, the trouble had started around 11:00pm when Amy was spotted going out onto the street to speak with a young woman whose identity remained unknown. She was said to have hugged the mystery woman before returning to her room alone, and it was 'within hours' that the other guests had heard raised voices and clattering furniture, followed by piercing screams, emanating from the room. A concierge had gone up to the couple's room, where 'Ms Winehouse, who has a history of self-harming, had asked for medical assistance to patch up cuts on her arm'.

> **Amy had the beginnings of a black eye, a scratch or cut near her eyebrow, and her left wrist and arm bound with plasters.**

That morning's edition of the *Daily Star* carried a photograph of the seriously bedraggled couple on its front page. Amy had the beginnings of a black eye, a scratch or cut near her eyebrow, and her left wrist and arm bound with plasters, while Blake had so many criss-cross slash marks on his face and neck that anyone might've thought he'd been given an Indian head-massage by Edward Scissorhands. Accompanying the photo was a report in which 'an onlooker' told the paper: 'Amy hit a few bars and was knocking back strawberry daiquiris like there was no tomorrow. Then she was wondering through the streets looking like a sad cross between a homeless child and a bag lady.' So, the anonymous source wasn't so much a casual onlooker as Amy's shadow?

Showbiz gossip columnist Perez Hilton (born Mario Armando Lavandeira Jr) got in on the act, writing on his entertainment blog, in what would prove to be a chilling piece of prescient journalism: 'Fuck the bullshit! Amy Winehouse is going to die if she continues down this destructive path!' Perez ended his blog by saying, 'We do believe in God and we pray that He is able to save Amy from death, which she keeps inviting into her life. And ditch that loser husband!'

Hilton's next blog update, later that same day, said that he'd sent Amy a text, and Amy had replied: 'Blake is the best man in the world. We would never ever harm each other. Take back what you said on the blog. I thought you was my girl. I was cutting myself after he found me in our room about to do drugs with a call girl and rightly

*Unhappy endings: An inebriated Amy wanders the streets of Camden during Blake's imprisonment, February 2008.*

*Bottle blonde: Amy leaves Blake's plea hearing at Snaresbrook Crown Court in January 2008 (left), and (right) lashes out at paparazzi waiting outside her home after being refused entry to visit Blake in Pentonville Prison, May 2008.*

said I wasn't good enough for him. I lost it and he saved my life.' Was the call girl Amy referred to the mystery woman lurking outside the Sanderson Hotel?

Over the course of the day, Amy sent Perez further text messages, each one pleading with him to remove the comment about ditching Blake from the blog. The first text read: 'For the last time he did not and never has hurt me. Say I told you what happened on your blog. He has such a hard time and he [is] so supportive . . . Please make amends. Kiss. Amy.' Amy's last message read: 'Please can you put up the truthful version straight away? It's bad enough that it's been there that long. I know you love me but he deserves the truth, he is an amazing man who saved my life again and got cut badly for his troubles. All he get's [sic] is horrible stories printed about him and he just keeps quiet, but this is too much. I'll be alright. I need to fight my man's corner for him though. Thanks girl. Amy.'

♪ ♪ ♪

In order to escape the media glare, Amy and Blake decamped to the Caribbean where they holidayed – or hid from the world, depending on one's point of view – in Saint

Lucia, at the exclusive £1,000-a-night Jade Mountain resort. But though the main protagonists had fled the stage, the media was perfectly content to turn its attention to the supporting actors, and the *Sun* carried an article in which Mitch Winehouse said seeing the photographs had left him feeling suicidal, while Giles Civil told the same paper, 'They [Amy and Blake] are going through abject denial at the moment. They don't see themselves as having a problem and are quite aggressive in defence of themselves. They believe they are recreational drug users but it seems this is not the case and clearly they are addicts.'

The following day's *Daily Mail* reported that Giles and Blake's mum Georgette had appeared on the BBC's *Radio Five Live* publicly calling for Amy's fans to boycott her records and to stop playing her music in a bid to stop them from killing themselves with drugs. And harking back to the Sanderson Hotel incident, the paper said that the pink ballet shoes Amy had been wearing that night were stained red with blood

> 'At some point, they are going to reach rock bottom and at that point, they will say, I don't want to do that anymore.'
> – Giles Civil

from where she'd 'allegedly' injected heroin between her toes. During the interview, Giles – who, it has to be said, was coping admirably with being centre stage – said that anyone with drug experience knew there was little point in sectioning Amy and Blake, or locking them up. 'At some point,' he added sombrely, 'they are going to reach rock bottom and at that point, they will say, I don't want to do that anymore.'

So that he wouldn't feel left out, the following day's edition of the *Sun* carried a second interview with Mitch in which he said he was going to his father's grave every day to pray for his wayward daughter, as he believed only 'divine intervention' could now save her. And in a thinly veiled attack against his son-in-law, Mitch added that Amy's self-harming and drug abuse had only started after marrying Blake.

On Tuesday 4 September, the 2007 Mercury Music Prize ceremony was staged at the Grosvenor House Hotel in London, where *Back to Black* was up against albums from the likes of Dizzee Rascal, Arctic Monkeys, Bat for Lashes, and winners on the night, the Klaxons. Against all expectations, Amy gave a spectacular acoustic performance of 'Love Is a Losing Game' that silenced the room, and while she might not have won, she must have been pleased to be back in the spotlight for all the right reasons.

The previous day's papers had all carried harrowing tales of Amy supposedly using heroin whilst away on her Caribbean break. But on being questioned at the ceremony by *London Lite*, Amy, looking tanned and relaxed, said, 'I feel really well at the moment. I had a great holiday with Blake, and I really don't know what the fuss was about.'

However, Amy's next appearance in London's free paper, on Thursday 20 September, was rather less favourable. 'Amy's a wreck at the Mobos', ran the headline that followed her shambling appearance at the previous evening's Mobo Awards, staged at the O2 Arena. This was the first time Amy had been on a stage with her band since the Lollapalooza Festival at the beginning of August, but those in the audience could have been forgiven for thinking they'd never even rehearsed together before. The confident Amy of a fortnight earlier was nowhere to be seen as she stumbled her way through 'Tears Dry on Their Own', and 'Me and Mr Jones'. Indeed, so inept was her performance during the latter song that at times it seemed as though she was following a different rhythm to the one the band was playing. One of the band, who, unsurprisingly, insisted on remaining anonymous, told the paper that Amy's drinking was the lesser of her two evils, because at least then she was only drunk, as opposed to drunk and stoned. 'If she'd have been on drugs tonight,' the player added warily, 'things could have been a whole lot worse.' Yet despite her onstage shortcomings, Amy beat off competition from Beverley Knight, Corrine Bailey Rae and Joss Stone to scoop the Best UK Female award. That same evening, she also picked up the Best Female Performer award at the Vodafone Live Music Awards ceremony staged at Earl's Court.

If the Earl's Court crowd were feeling peeved that Amy only put in an appearance to collect her gong, those gathered inside the Grosvenor House Hotel at the *Q* Awards the following month had to settle for Mark Ronson going up to accept the Best Album award on Amy's behalf. That the award eventually arrived in Camden at all was something of a miracle, as Ronson inadvertently left it behind on leaving Bar Soho on Old Compton Street, where he'd allegedly partied until the early hours.

♪♪♪

When the news broke that Amy would be cancelling her US tour dates, many of the ticket-holders for her European tour – which was set to commence nine days after the final American date in Boston – expressed concern that these dates could suffer the same fate. But they needn't have worried, as Amy took to the Tempodrom stage in Berlin on Monday 15 October showing little or no sign of the troubles that had been plaguing her all summer. Whilst Amy was in the German capital, Mark Ronson's label Columbia released his and Amy's collaborative cover of the Zutons' 'Valerie', which featured on his recently-released *Versions* album. The single would climb all the way to number 2 on the UK chart, but while the song is undoubtedly catchy in its own right, it's Amy's remarkable vocal that brings the lyric to life.

Following on from a show at the Congress Centrum CCH 3 in Hamburg the following evening, the tour moved directly onto Copenhagen, the Danish capital,

*The downward spiral: Amy onstage during a shambolic performance at the 2007 Mobo Awards.*

where a show at the Store Vega also passed without incident. Then it was across the border into Norway, where Amy was set to appear at the Grieghallen in Bergen the following evening. But just when things appeared to be running smoothly, the Thursday 19 October edition of *London Lite* reported that Amy and Blake had been arrested by city police at around 7:00pm the previous evening for suspected drug possession. It appeared that police had received a call from staff at the Hotel Norge, where the tour party was staying, after smelling marijuana smoke coming from Amy's room. According to the paper's sources, Amy and Blake were each fined £350 for possession, and released sometime during the early hours of Friday morning. 'She spent a few hours in custody from Thursday evening to early Friday, she got a fine and then she was released,' prosecutor Lars Morten Lothe told the press. 'She paid the fine, so this thing is over for us now.' After a show at the Sentrum Scene in Oslo that same evening, the tour wended its way to Amsterdam, where Amy was due to play the Heineken Music Hall. Here, of course, she and Blake were free to puff away on the green without any fear of official interruption.

> **'I have taken pills for depression, but they slowed me down. I believe there are lots of people who have these mood changes.'**
> – Amy Winehouse

On Tuesday 24 October, the tour returned to Germany for a show at the Muffathalle in Munich, before crossing the border into Switzerland. Whilst Amy making her Swiss debut, the *Daily Mail* published an interview she'd given to the German magazine *Stern* the previous afternoon. In the interview Amy spoke about her recent struggles with depression, and her feeling there was a black cloud constantly hanging over her. 'I have taken pills for depression, but they slowed me down,' she said. 'I believe there are lots of people who have these mood changes.'

The tour then crossed the Alps into Italy for the first of two shows in Milan at the Rolling Stone Club on Friday 26 October. Then, following a show at Alcatraz, Amy was back in Germany playing at the Palladium in Cologne. The tour's penultimate date was at Le Zenith in Paris on Monday 29 October, where fans reported another erratic performance, and the following night Amy brought the curtain down with a show at the Ancienne Belgique in Brussels.

Two nights later Amy was back in Munich at the MTV Europe Music Video Awards, where she performed 'Back to Black', and collected the much-coveted Artists' Choice award.

♪ ♪ ♪

*You take me higher: Amy and Blake backstage at the MTV Europe Music Awards in Munich, Germany, November 2007.*

An eighteen-date UK tour was set to commence in two weeks with a show at the 13,000-capacity National Indoor Arena, on Wednesday 14 November, so Island decided to milk the cash cow by releasing a deluxe edition of *Back to Black* with a bonus disc featuring miscellaneous rare recordings and live tracks, as well as the *I Told You I Was Trouble: Amy Winehouse Live in London* DVD, which was filmed back in May at one of the rescheduled Shepherd's Bush Empire shows. Four days later, the fireworks went off for real when a *Daily Mirror* 'World Exclusive' reported that Blake had been arrested by a team of plain-clothed detectives and led away from Amy's Camden flat in handcuffs. According to the Mirror, the early-morning arrest was in connection with Blake's suspected attempts to pervert the course of justice by fixing his impending trial, which was scheduled for that coming Monday. Back in June, Blake and his associate Michael Brown were alleged to have assaulted a barman at the Macbeth pub in Hoxton, east London, and were set to answer the assault charge.

> **Not only did she struggle to remember the words to the songs, she appeared incapable of holding her guitar, let alone playing it, and was even reported to have fallen over at one point.**

When photographs of a despondent Amy standing outside Pentonville Prison, where Blake was being held, began doing the rounds, her UK fans must have feared the worst. But rather than sit around moping in the east London flat where she'd been staying following Blake's incarceration, Amy took the stoic approach that the show must go on. However, it might have better for all concerned if she hadn't. According to reports, the Birmingham show was an unmitigated disaster. After keeping the expectant NIA audience waiting an hour before coming onstage looking completely the worse for wear, she lumbered about stage like a somnambulistic scarecrow. Not only did she struggle to remember the words to the songs, she appeared incapable of holding her guitar, let alone playing it, and was even reported to have fallen over at one point. It might have been funny had the audience come to see alternative comedy, but they'd paid their hard-earned money to see the woman reputed to be the best female vocalist of her generation, and slowly but surely a ring of boos began to rise up around the hall. While the booing and catcalls brought a reaction from Amy, it wasn't the one the audience had been expecting. 'Let me tell you something,' she retorted. 'First of all, if you're booing you're a mug for buying a ticket. Second, to all those booing, just wait till my husband gets out of incarceration. And I mean that.' And after calling the crowd 'monkey cunts', she hurled the microphone to the floor and stormed from the stage.

The tabloids went into overdrive in their collective condemnation of Amy's onstage antics, but the *Times* appeared, if not forgiving, then at least sympathetic

*Pale and waiflike, Amy walks through London's Covent Garden in August 2007.*

to Amy's plight. 'Even by her normal soap-opera standards, this last fortnight has been unusually turbulent for Amy Winehouse.' After drolly citing the fact that Blake was languishing behind bars, coupled with a tumultuous year of headline-grabbing arrests, drug confessions, public fights, and family strife, and managing to get in the by now ubiquitous rehab joke, the review gave an overview of her shambolic showing in the second city, and made inevitable comparisons to Pete Doherty, whose own drug predilections were taking up more column inches than his obvious songwriting talents. The paper then attempted to show the differences between the two performers by saying that unlike Doherty, Amy's career appeared to 'have gained extra momentum from her backstage troubles, rather than being hobbled by them'. Though it's unlikely that any of the 13,000 souls who'd gathered within the NIA the previous night, to witness Amy's latest falling from the bar stool, would be in agreement.

After mentioning that *Back to Black* had recently been confirmed as the biggest-selling UK album of the year, the review theorised that Amy's bad-girl antics had 'added an extra dash of Edith Piaf-style authenticity to all those fabulously overcooked 1950s tramp-vamp lyrics about bruised hearts, toxic addictions, men behaving badly and women behaving worse'. As in previous reviews, the *Times* felt compelled to question the choice of venue, which had again appeared to overwhelm Amy at times. 'The fetchingly sloppy, intimate delivery that works a treat in smaller clubs does not translate well to arenas and some of her bouncy retro-soul hits fell a little flat.'

Worse was to follow, because while the tour was wending its way up to Glasgow, where Amy was set to perform two shows over consecutive nights at Glasgow's Barrowlands on 16 and 17 November, the *NME* – having picked up the Amy battering-baton from the *Sun* – ran a story saying that Amy's tour manager Thom Stone had quit the tour because Amy had supposedly been smoking heroin on the tour bus. According to the *NME*'s report, the medical tests Stone had undertaken to see if any heroin traces were showing in his bloodstream had tested positive. And as he was a non-user himself, the only way the drug could have entered his bloodstream was through passive smoking. Further evidence that Amy was using came courtesy of YouTube, on which a video clip taken during Amy's performance in Zurich the previous month was posted, where she can be seen retrieving a small sachet of powder – purported to be either heroin or cocaine – that she'd secreted within her beehive and proceeding to snort it whilst onstage.

♪ ♪ ♪

With the media once again concentrating on the heroin rather than the heroine, those closest to Amy must have been on tenterhooks, expecting her to crumble at any given moment. Yet the following night's show at the Newcastle Academy received

*Lookin' up: Amy fixes her hair in a car's rear-view mirror before travelling to visit Blake in prison, March 2008.*

glowing reviews. The *Guardian* opined that Amy's voice was a 'roar of jazz and blues' as she effortlessly reeled off tracks from *Back to Black*. Whilst confessing to having taken his seat in the balcony fearing the worst, the broadsheet's reviewer was pleased to be able to fire off a positive missive. 'The performance is so eerily fantastic that you end up looking for telltale flaws.' The only flaw of the evening – at least in the reviewer's eyes – came with what he saw as Amy's 'ongoing obsession with covering her cleavage' after she'd inadvertently exposed her bra whilst removing her guitar. Nevertheless, he felt compelled to cite the performance as 'an absorbing example of a singer living every lyric'.

> **'Most people who are hooked on heroin don't have anything else in their life, but Amy has her music, her career, and a loving family.'** – Janis Winehouse

But such constructive critiques would inevitably prove to be yet another false dawn, as the day after her show at Blackpool's Empress Ballroom two days later, news of a fresh drug scandal involving Amy was in circulation. That day's *Evening Standard* carried a photo of Amy arriving at the Lancashire seaside resort with what the paper termed 'a suspicious trace of a powdered substance' visible in her right nostril. Not to be outdone, the *Sun* covered the story under the punning headline 'Amy Goes Back to White'. Having highlighted the essential ingredients making up Amy's pitiable existence, such as Blake being banged-up, her mum being pleased her hubby was inside, and her fans booing her from the stage – which might have pushed Amy back to the 'white' – while being careful not to draw any conclusions as to what the white powder lodged in Amy's nose might be, the paper concluded by saying that the latest damning photo of Amy suggested she was still struggling in her battle against her drug demons.

The following week's edition of the women's-only *First* magazine carried an exclusive interview with Janis Winehouse in which Amy's mum reiterated her delight at Blake being behind bars. Interviewed at the London flat she shared with her partner of seven years, Tony, and where Amy's Mobo trophy, Elle *Style* award, and a double-platinum disc for *Back to Black* took pride of place, Janis spoke of her anguish at going public about her daughter being better off with Blake in prison. 'While they are apart, she will wake up and think, "What have I done?"' And while she readily recognised Amy's love for Blake, Janis added, 'If the relationship is meant to be, it will survive this. But Amy's got to love him for him, not because she feels sorry for him or because he's got her doped up.'

Speaking about the day Blake was arrested, Janis said she and Tony were due to head over to Camden to visit Amy and Blake (which, as she'd been diagnosed with multiple sclerosis around the time of *Frank*'s release, wasn't without its inherent difficulties), when Amy had called to ask them not to come to the flat, saying that

*Family ties: Amy and her mother Janis celebrate her Grammy Awards success in February 2008 (left), and (right) Amy hugs her father Mitch outside one of his London concerts in October 2010.*

she'd meet them at a nearby pub instead. Soon afterwards, Amy had called again asking to be picked up in Hackney. Of course, Amy acting strange was nothing out of the ordinary, but Janis was mystified as to what her daughter was doing in Hackney – especially as the day wore on without Amy responding to any of her calls or texts. Indeed, it was only when Amy's brother Alex had called to say the police had conducted a raid on the flat and arrested Blake that the mystery was cleared up. While Janis confessed to never having directly broached the subject of drugs with Amy (she hadn't been at the Four Seasons Hotel summit meeting back in August), she said she knew from what others close to Amy had told her that Amy had talked about therapy, and desperately wanted to get herself cleaned up. Though it might have been somewhat naive of her, given what was being written about her daughter on a near-daily basis, Janis said Amy hadn't been doing drugs for a long enough period to become addicted: 'Most people who are hooked on heroin don't have anything else in their life, but Amy has her music, her career, and a loving family.'

When *First* magazine hit the newsstands, Amy had put in two solid performances at the 5,000-capacity Brixton Academy over November 22 and 23, before faltering badly again a day later at the HMV Hammersmith Apollo. According to the *NME*'s blow-by-blow ringside report, Amy had been some forty-five minutes late going onstage, by which time some sections of the audience had already been demanding their money back, only to wander offstage again midway through the set, leaving one of her back-up singers to pick up the reins. Though she soon returned, the reviewer noted that Amy had appeared to be unstable on her feet, as though her backstage pick-me-up wasn't on general prescription. She lasted until the encore, but left the stage again midway through 'Valerie', this time for good. Once again her bemused backing singers were forced to take over vocal duties.

At the subsequent show at the Brighton Centre on 26 November, despite keeping the crowd waiting some forty minutes before appearing from behind the curtain, Amy managed to get through the set with only a couple of unscheduled breaks. The crowd held its collective breath in anticipation of witnessing Amy's latest meltdown, and when she disappeared from the stage entirely, certain sections of the crowd suspected that she'd returned to the dressing room for a pick-me-up, but she returned a few minutes later looking no worse for wear and, having completed the hour-long set, came on again for an unexpected encore. However, the Brighton encore would prove to be the tour's swansong, for the following evening – just two hours before the doors were due to open at Bournemouth's International Centre – it was announced that this and the remaining eight dates were now cancelled. A spokesperson subsequently told the media, 'Amy Winehouse has cancelled all remaining live and promotional appearances for the remainder of the year on the instruction of her doctor. The rigours involved in touring and the intense emotional strain that Amy has been under in recent weeks have taken their toll. In the interests of her health and well-being, Amy has been ordered to take complete rest and deal with her health issues. Refunds for the remaining dates will be issued from the point of purchase.' In light of the cancellations, the *Times* calculated that although the refunds for the cancelled nine shows would cost an estimated £500,000, the tour had been set to gross £1.25million, so Amy was still in pocket.

And while her spokesperson said the cancellations were down to health issues, the real reason was that Amy was pining for her man. 'I can't give it my all onstage without my Blake,' she told the *Daily Mirror* that same week. 'I'm so sorry, but I don't want to do the shows half-heartedly. I love singing but my husband is everything to me and without him it's not the same.'

♪♪♪

Amy might have taken herself off the market, but with Christmas fast approaching, on Monday 10 December Island released 'Love Is a Losing Game', backed with a Kardinal Beats mix of the title track – the fifth single to be culled from *Back to*

*Black*. But while it's undoubtedly one of the best songs in the Winehouse canon, your average British consumer recognises the sound of a barrel being scraped when they hear it, and the single stalled at a lowly number 46.

On a more positive note, sales of the parent album had now reached an unbelievable 4.5 million copies worldwide, and were showing little sign of slowing down. In early December, the news came through that Amy had received no less than six nominations at the forthcoming Fiftieth Grammy Awards: Album of the Year, Record of the Year, Best Female Vocal Performance, Best New Artist, Best Pop Vocal Album and Song of the Year. The ceremony was set to take place at the Staples Centre in Los Angeles on Sunday, 10 February 2008, and if Amy were to win all six categories she would be the first artist to do so.

> **'I can't give it my all onstage without my Blake. I'm so sorry, but I don't want to do the shows half-heartedly. I love singing but my husband is everything to me and without him it's not the same.'** – Amy Winehouse

On the home front, Amy left Camden and moved in with friends in Hackney. It was widely reported that she was looking to buy a new home as part of a new start, and photographs appeared of her doing the usual mundane things that everyone else does, such as getting late-night takeaways and shopping for groceries. Family and friends began to hope, but those hopes were dashed forever when a photo of an anguished Amy wandering the Hackney streets barefoot in the freezing November night, clad in only a red bra and jeans, with a crucifix about her neck, appeared in the tabloids. For behind the millions of records sold, the accolades and awards, the accompanying showbiz glitz and glamour, within that naked, single-frame snapshot, the tragedy of Amy Winehouse's life was laid bare for all the world to see. And it didn't make for pretty viewing.

Little was seen of Amy over the Christmas period, but on Friday, 25 January 2008, the *Guardian* reported that Amy had finally said yes, yes, yes, and gone into rehab the previous day. But according to the paper, her acquiescence wasn't because of any soul-searching introspection, or influence from her family during the festive season, but rather because video footage had surfaced of her smoking crack cocaine. Though there was no word from Amy or her family in the article, Amy's label was quoted as saying, 'She [Amy] has come to understand that she requires specialist treatment to continue her ongoing recovery from drug addiction.' When the news broke, everyone assumed Amy was at the Priory, but the following day the *Daily Mirror* announced that she was in fact receiving treatment at the Capio Nightingale clinic in central London.

# 10. A Wounded Thing Must Hide

'To be honest, my husband's away, I'm bored, I'm young. I felt like there was nothing to live for. It's just been a low ebb.'

Of course, while the world was sighing collective relief that Amy was finally seeking the professional help she so obviously needed, her admission to hospital raised the question of whether she'd be able to appear and perform at the Grammy Awards, which were now just a couple of weeks way. Five days before the ceremony, Amy left hospital to visit the US Embassy in Grosvenor Square to apply for a visa. But while those in authority at the US Immigration Office were appreciative of her talent, they were less thrilled about her overt drug use, and two days later the news broke that Amy's visa application had been declined. The following day, the *Daily Telegraph*, commenting on the decision, quoted from a statement issued by Amy's publicity team: 'Although disappointed with the decision [Amy] has accepted the ruling and will be concentrating on her recovery. Amy has been treated well and fairly by the [US] embassy staff and thanks everyone for the support in trying to make this happen. There will of course be other opportunities and she very much looks forward to visiting America in the near future.'

On the Friday before the ceremony it was announced that Amy would be performing live via satellite, but it seemed that she had friends in higher places than she'd imagined, as later that day the US Embassy overturned its decision and announced it would now be granting her a visa. Yet, despite this eleventh-hour u-turn, Amy announced she would stick with her initial decision to perform 'Rehab' and 'You Know I'm No Good' via satellite from the Riverside Studios in London, and her US publicist subsequently issued the following statement: 'Unfortunately, due to the logistics involved and timing complications, Amy will not be coming to the US this weekend to perform at the Grammys in Los Angeles.'

*Amy appears strung-out onstage at the V Festival in August 2008. 'I get my nuts off sometimes,' she told* Rolling Stone. *'But it's never been like, "Amy, get your life together."'*

Amy also told the *Times*, 'I'm raring to go and really excited to be performing at my first Grammy Awards. I'd like to thank everyone for their support over the last couple of weeks. I'm really sorry I can't be there but I appreciate that I'm being given a second chance via satellite.'

On the night, Amy was expected to pick up three of the six awards for which she'd been nominated. The pundits were predicting she'd pip Taylor Swift to the post for Best New Artist, as well as fend off stiff competition from Christina Aguilera ('Candyman'), Fergie ('Big Girls Don't Cry') and Nelly Furtado ('Say It Right') in the Best Female Pop Vocalist category. And though Maroon 5's *It Won't Be Soon Before Long* had been accruing accolades, it was expected that *Back to Black* would win the Best Pop Vocal Album award.

However, when it came to the more prestigious honours, the pundits were convinced that Rihanna's 'Umbrella' would triumph over 'Rehab' in both the Best Record and Best Song categories, while Kanye West's *Graduation* was odds-on favourite for Best Album, and the surprise of the night came when the award went instead to Herbie Hancock's *River: The Joni Letters*.

> **'I am so proud of this album. I put my heart and soul into it and it's wicked to be recognised in this way. I feel truly honoured to be mentioned in the same breath as many of the artists present tonight and to win is even more amazing.' – Amy Winehouse**

Winning five Grammys at a single sitting placed Amy alongside Lauryn Hill, Alicia Keys, Norah Jones and Beyoncé. (Beyoncé would claim the crown outright by winning six awards in 2010.) *Back to Black* was still hovering in the upper reaches of the *Billboard* 200, and following Amy's multi-Grammy-Award-winning evening, the album shot up from number 24 to number 2.

'I am so proud of this album [*Back to Black*],' a buoyant Amy told the *Daily Telegraph* the day after the ceremony. 'I put my heart and soul into it and it's wicked to be recognised in this way. I feel truly honoured to be mentioned in the same breath as many of the artists present tonight and to win is even more amazing.' It's worth remembering that while such platitudes are standard fare from award recipients, Amy was never one to give credit where it wasn't due.

While winning the Record of the Year award, Amy predictably dedicated her win to her mum and dad, and to her 'Blake incarcerated'. But she also proudly declared, 'This is for London, because Camden Town is burning down' – a reference to the fire that ravaged her local pub the Hawley Arms and much of Camden Market on the night of her Grammys success.

Alex Winehouse, who usually kept his own council were his kid sister was involved, told the *Times*, 'It was without a shadow of a doubt the greatest night our family has enjoyed in a long, long time. If I told you she sounded good in rehearsals, then

*Amy won five awards at the 2008 Grammys (left), as well as (right) the 2008 Ivor Novello award for Best Song Musically and Lyrically, for 'Love Is a Losing Game'.*

her live performance was truly from another planet. It was an electrically charged performance that sent kilowatts through the audience. Never mind that it was four in the morning – the place was literally jumping, with all thoughts of sleep forgotten.'

Alex also knew his sister well enough to know when she was faking it, but believed her reaction to winning the Best Record award was both genuine and truly moving. 'For the first time in God only knows how long, my parents were truly happy, and Amy was too. So of course was I. We hugged and kissed, and suddenly the world melted away; we were alone, a loving family that has suffered so much and – we deeply wish – come out the other side.'

It was a night dad Mitch would also treasure. 'The greatest story for me was the night she [Amy] had her big Grammy win,' he told *OK!* magazine in August 2011. 'She never gets excited about anything. But the night she won five Grammys the last one was presented by Tony Bennett. She couldn't believe it – what a night!'

To go with the five Grammys, Amy also received a standing ovation from the star-studded throng gathered within the Staples Centre, but once the spotlight had faded she returned alone to the Capio Nightingale clinic for her ongoing treatment.

♪ ♪ ♪

On Tuesday 20 February, Amy attended the Brit Awards, where she performed 'Valerie' with Mark Ronson, and 'Love Is a Losing Game'. 'Valerie' had been nominated for Best British Single, but the trophy went to Take That's 'Shine', and though Ronson picked up the Best British Male award, Amy went home empty-handed. By this time, she had left hospital, and moved back to Camden, where she was renting a secluded mews property on one of the borough's more peaceful streets.

With Amy out of rehab, and appearing to be on the mend, the question on everybody's lips was when she would return to the studio to start work on a new album. The answer came sometime in late March, when the *NME* reported that Amy was working on new material, and that the songs already written were 'very dark', with many of them 'themed around the subject of death'. The paper also claimed that Amy would soon be flying out to the Bahamas to begin work on the album, and that she would once again be teaming up with producer Salaam Remi. However, a couple of weeks later, the sessions were cancelled without reason, which left little hope of the mooted new album appearing before 2009.

However, good news arrived in the third week of April when Amy learned that she'd been nominated for three Ivor Novello awards, which would be announced at the annual ceremony on 20 May, staged once again at the Grosvenor House Hotel on Park Lane. Both 'Love Is a Losing Game' and 'You Know I'm No Good' were nominated in the Best Song Musically and Lyrically category, while 'Rehab' was listed in the Best Selling British Song category.

While everything had gone quiet in regard to Amy recording her third album, news emerged that she was in the studio with Mark Ronson, collaborating on a possible theme tune for the new James Bond film, *Quantum of Solace*. The couple had already recorded a version of Lesley Gore's 1963 hit 'It's My Party' for the Quincy Jones tribute album, *Q: Soul Bossa Nostra*, and Ronson told the media: 'They [the studio] asked Amy, and I think Amy said that if she did it, she'd want to do it with me. So hopefully, something will come of it. The demo sounds like a James Bond theme, hopefully. But I don't know if it'll get used.'

Yet according to the *NME*, following up on an article which had first appeared in the *Sun*, Amy and Ronson had fallen out during the recording sessions at Ronson's home studio in Henley, because of Amy's 'erratic behaviour'. Ronson told the music magazine, 'We did work on it [the song] but we never finished it. I don't think it will happen unless by some miracle it gets recorded and someone sings on it. I'm not sure Amy is ready to work on music yet.'

Metropolis attempted to play down the rift by issuing the following statement: 'Mark presented a track to Amy, but she had other ideas about the direction it should

*Mark Ronson and Amy perform their cover of the Zutons' 'Valerie' live onstage at the 2008 Brit Awards. The single was a huge chart success.*

take. We're sure they will continue to make great music together.' But Amy took Ronson's innocuous comment about her not being ready to heart and for a time the two didn't speak.

The job of writing the theme tune for *Quantum of Solace* was subsequently given to Jack Black from the White Stripes, and the resultant song, 'Another Way to Die', was recorded by Black and Alicia Keys.

Amy's fallouts weren't only restricted to the recording studio, however, and sometime during the early hours of Tuesday 23 April, Amy – having allegedly been chasing the dragon during a six-hour bender – got embroiled in a fracas outside a Camden pub when she allegedly head-butted a passer-by, whose only crime was to hail a 'disorientated-looking' Amy a taxi. According to the following day's edition of the *Daily Mail*, Amy was also alleged to have punched Moroccan musician Mustapha el Mounmi in the face simply because he was he was unwilling to give up the pool table in another Camden pub. The paper finished by saying that if convicted, Amy faced up to six months in prison, and a £2,000 fine. Had the reporters who beat a trail to Camden

> 'Now is the time to exert whatever pressure we have to try to do it. I've told them she is a danger to herself. There is evidence of self-harming and she is a danger to other people because she's attacked someone.' – Mitch Winehouse

that night thought to interview Amy's friends, they would have heard how she was often targeted by supposedly innocent 'passers-by', who would pester her for an autograph, a word, or something more until her patience finally snapped. But in the jaundiced glare of the press, only tales of Amy Winehouse either drunk or on drugs were headline fare.

Two days later, Amy walked into Holborn police station and voluntarily gave herself up for questioning in connection with the incidents. The *Daily Telegraph* reported that Amy had been 'cautioned for common assault after spending the night in a cell in a central London police station'. In a formal statement issued by her manager Raye Cosbert, Amy admitted to the common assault charge – she had slapped the man with her open hand – and accepted the caution. As a result of her being fully co-operative with the police's enquiries, no further action would be taken.

The police may have had no further interest in Amy, but the day after she was released from custody, the 27 April edition of the *News of the World* carried an exclusive interview with her dad Mitch under the headline: 'Dad Calls for Amy Winehouse to Be Sectioned'. It seemed Mitch had reached the end of his tether with his daughter, and, having explored all the available options, believed the only way to save Amy from killing herself with drugs was to have her sectioned under the Mental Health

*Been smoking too long: Amy steps out for a cigarette during a visit to a Caribbean restaurant in Soho, London, February 2008.*

Act. 'Now is the time to exert whatever pressure we have to try to do it. I've told them she is a danger to herself. There is evidence of self-harming and she is a danger to other people because she's attacked someone.'

Her mother Janis, however, had resigned herself to the fact that her daughter was probably beyond earthly help. 'We're watching her kill herself slowly,' she told the press. 'It's like watching a car crash – this person throwing these gifts away. I've already come to terms with her dead. I've steeled myself to ask her on what ground she wants to be buried, in which cemetery.'

The irony wouldn't have been lost on those closest to Amy that on the day of Mitch's *News of the World* exclusive, the *Sunday Times* published its annual 'Britain's Rich List', which included Amy as a new entrant, with a personal fortune estimated at £10 million. Her bank balance received another sizeable boost when the Russian billionaire Roman Abramovich – who is best known in the UK for being the owner of Chelsea Football Club – paid her a staggering £1 million for performing a private one-off show at the glitzy inauguration of a new art gallery in Moscow, set up by his girlfriend, Daria Zhukova. Having flown in on Abramovich's private jet, Amy performed in front of 300 or so celebrities and figures from the art world at the Garage Gallery, which was said to be twice the size of the pitch at Stamford Bridge, and had formerly been used to house public transport. Nice work if you can get it.

♪♪♪

Though Amy didn't agree with her dad's prognosis that she should be 'sectioned', she was willing to admit she needed help to curb her addictions, and returned to the Capio Nightingale clinic for treatment. With the UK summer festival season fast approaching, on Friday 30 May, Amy flew out to Portugal to make what would be her first live appearance of the year at the Rock in Rio Lisboa Festival, which also featured Linkin Park, Metallica, Bon Jovi and Alanis Morisette on the bill. After keeping the sell-out, 90,000-strong crowd gathered inside the Parque de Bela Vista waiting for nearly an hour, when she finally took to the stage she stunned the crowd by saying it might have been better had she cancelled as her voice was feeling weak. She also appeared to be suffering from nerves, as she dropped the microphone and sipped wine throughout the performance. 'My voice isn't singing right, and I can't even hold the microphone,' she said by way of an apology after picking up the mic. 'But I wanted to be here so much.' Though it soon became apparent that her throat wasn't up to the task, she was determined to struggle on as best she could. After the concert, the reaction was one of anger and dismay, with many fans taking to the internet to insist that she needed either to quit drink and drugs, or stop performing altogether.

Despite having gone public with his claim that Amy should be sectioned for her own good, Mitch was there to support his daughter when she was diagnosed as showing signs of early-stage emphysema, and an irregular heartbeat, in early June. 'She's got

*Little ole wine drinker me: Amy takes a sip of Dutch courage onstage at the Rock in Rio Festival in Madrid, June 2008 (left) and (right) relaxes by the pool in Rio de Janeiro, Brazil, January 2011.*

emphysema,' Mitch told the *Sunday Mirror* that same month. 'It's in its early stages, but had it gone on for another month they painted a very vivid picture of her sitting there like an old person with [an oxygen] mask on her face struggling to breathe. When we got to the hospital a room was ready. Several doctors came in and checked to make sure she didn't need any emergency treatment. They put her on a drip straight away because she was dehydrated. She said, 'Don't worry about me, dad. I know I've got to stop taking drugs now.' At the hospital we found she'd been awake for forty-eight hours. We can only speculate she'd been taking drugs all that time. She curled up in bed and went to sleep. In between tests, she slept for almost three days solid.'

When rumours started doing the rounds about Amy's ailment being something more sinister, Mitch once again went public to put the record straight: 'There's been some confusing messages coming out,' he told Radio One's *Newsbeat*. 'There's been stuff about TB, stuff about HIV, but she hasn't got any of that. She has a small amount of emphysema. Obviously there's a hangover from the drugs situation but with no more inhalation from smoke of any kind, she'll be absolutely fine. That's the extent of her medical problems. It is scary, emphysema is scarring on the lungs and

*Amy onstage at Glastonbury Festival in June 2008 – during this performance, she was filmed punching an audience member in the front row.*

there is a small amount there. It hasn't gone too far, it's not irreparable. Really she can't even smoke anymore, let alone the other thing. With patience, her lungs will recover completely. She's responding really well to treatment, she's flourishing. The thing that's keeping her going is thought of being able to perform again. That's what she lives for and she really wants to do the gigs at the weekend, and with the doctors' permission – and they have given her permission – she will perform. The future for her and our family and her fans and the people that love her, is a lot brighter than it was. Things have really turned a corner. She's very intelligent and she knows what she needs to do and she's getting on with it.'

♪ ♪ ♪

The first of the weekend shows Mitch had alluded to was at the Nelson Mandela Ninetieth Birthday Tribute in Hyde Park on Friday 27 June, which formed part of the 46664 concerts to promote awareness of the HIV/AIDS pandemic (46664 had been Mandela's prison number whilst imprisoned on Robben Island). As a finale, at the end of the three-and-a-half-hour concert, Amy and ex-Specials keyboardist Jerry Dammers were joined onstage by the night's other performers – including Annie Lennox and Leona Lewis, the Sugarbabes, and the Soweto Gospel Choir – for a rendition of the Specials' 1984 hit 'Free Nelson Mandela', which Dammers had penned to raise awareness of Mandela's plight. The song's title also made up its anthemic chorus, but instead of singing along with the others, Amy cheekily amended the lyric to 'free Blakey my fella', much to the amusement of the crowd.

The following night Amy tottered onto the Pyramid Stage at Glastonbury in a tiny, blue-sequinned number and four-inch heels, with her beehive looking so ridiculously top-heavy that at times it seemed she might topple into the crowd. But given her recent turmoil, it was good to see her enjoying herself, belting out song after song in her own inimitable sultry style; making it all appear so effortless while cracking jokes, and yes, having the occasional tipple of red wine.

> '**The future for her and our family and her fans and the people that love her, is a lot brighter than it was. Things have really turned a corner. She's very intelligent and she knows what she needs to do and she's getting on with it.**' – Mitch Winehouse

After mildly chastising Amy for opting to scat her way through the set instead of singing, as well as appearing to thump an overzealous male at the front of the stage, the *Guardian* opined, 'Her set comprised mainly of the *Back to Black* classics, though none were executed with any lucidity or sense of rhythm. As with the rest of her performance, covers of the Specials' 'A Message to You Rudy', and 'Hey Little Rich Girl' were almost reduced to instrumentals as she neglected to use her most impressive asset, her voice.' Whilst reviewing Amy's previous Glastonbury outing, the paper had likened her to a 'rabbit caught in the headlights', and this year it thought the stunned expression had been replaced by one of fierce awareness. 'She knows exactly what people think and expect of her, and she loathes it. The main message of the night was an incoherent up yours to a crowd who, for the main part, just wanted to sing along to a version of "Valerie" that they recognised.'

Next up on the festival calendar was the second Rock in Rio Festival, staged in the Ciudad del Rock in south-east Madrid, on Friday 4 July. Amy put in another solid performance by all accounts, but the demons that had plagued her year returned with a 'V for vengeance' at the V Festival weekend of 16 and 17 August. 'Amy Winehouse is back to her worst after two V Festival gigs in two nights,' said the *Daily Mail*, while, 'Amy Winehouse is pants again at V Festival' was the *Mirror*'s damning verdict. According to those who witnessed both events, Amy's performance at Stafford on the Saturday – where she arrived late onstage and seemingly without knickers – was pitiful. Though she cleaned up both herself and her act in time for Sunday's outing in Chelmsford, it was definitely a case of way too little, coming way too late. The *Daily Mail* wrote of her Essex show: 'Amy was still smarting from the boos her Saturday night performance had earned her. Her stuttering performance saw hordes of fans stream away from the main stage. She told the crowd: "You're a really nuts crowd. I'm not on drugs, honest. So boo you guys for yesterday."'

Having pulled out of the Rock en Seine Festival for the second year running due to 'illness', Amy had a couple of weeks' breathing space to sort herself out in time for her next scheduled appearance at the Isle of Wight's Bestival on Saturday 6 September. But once again, Amy proved her own worst enemy, and played right into her detractors' hands. According to the *NME*, Amy arrived onstage forty minutes late, which meant she was forced to truncate her set to just thirty-five minutes. This didn't go down too well with the 30,000 hardy souls who had endured appalling weather conditions to see her play during the rain-soaked weekend.

♪ ♪ ♪

Perhaps not surprisingly, Amy kept something of a low profile for the remainder of 2008, but shortly before Christmas she flew out to Saint Lucia, the same Caribbean island where she and Blake had taken their honeymoon the previous year. What had initially been intended as a relaxing break, however, stretched to an eighteen-month extended stay. Though her friends and family were missing her, they were happy that she was now far away enough from the drug dealers who haunted her world, and had a real chance of cleaning up. Her label was also pleased with Amy's relocation, and so desperate were they for their troubled star to get back to making music that they arranged for a portable studio and a producer to be flown out to the island. 'The album will be six months at the most,' Amy told *Rolling Stone* in July 2010. 'It's going to be very much the same as my second album, where there's a lot of jukebox stuff and songs that are . . . just jukebox, really.'

Amy may have been drug-free, but alcohol remained very much a weakness, and the recording sessions soon gave way to afternoons lounging by the pool drinking rum cocktails. Holidaymakers at the nearby five-star LeSport Hotel got used to seeing Amy sitting at the bar, barefoot and unwashed and downing tequila shots for breakfast. She was reportedly hospitalised on several occasions during her stay, and though Mitch went out to see her, he returned within days, telling reporters that only Amy could save herself. Further proof that Amy's drink problems were getting steadily worse came with her shambolic headline appearance at the island's annual jazz festival at the historic Pigeon Island National Park in May 2009.

The *Daily Telegraph* was particularly scathing in its comments: 'Despite hopes that

*Amy stands in front of a Union Jack flag during her DJ set at the Camden Monarch in July 2008. She played records by artists including the Supremes and Curtis Mayfield.*

her prolonged stay on the Caribbean island of Saint Lucia would have rid Amy Winehouse of her demons, it was clear from the moment she took to the stage at the island's annual jazz festival at the weekend that they were alive and kicking.'

The broadsheet went on to say that Amy had looked unsure and unsteady on her feet, and that when she approached the microphone for the opening number 'Know You Now', her voice had lacked both power and conviction. Midway through 'Some Unholy War' she brought the proceedings to an unceremonious halt on account of her being bored. While the paper was willing to concede that there were occasional glimpses of Amy's Grammy Award-winning voice, for the most part it was shaky and strangely strained. It seemed her vocal inadequacy was matched by her increasingly peculiar stage antics – aside from greedily swigging down 'a steady supply of drinks', she repeatedly raised her skimpy dress to 'expose her knickers'.

Further dramas came in the form of a heavy downpour and a lighting failure, which resulted in two songs being sung in total darkness. Even her usually supportive backing band appeared unsure of what to do when, midway through 'Valerie' – which turned out to be the final song – she walked offstage and failed to return, an act which earned a chorus of boos from the island's disillusioned inhabitants, for whom the $50 entrance fee represented a substantial amount of their monthly earnings.

> ### 'I'll deal with Blake when I get back. Our whole marriage was based on drugs.' – Amy Winehouse

Amy's management – in what could only be described as a damage limitation exercise – issued a statement saying that the concert had been shortened because the storm that caused the temporary lighting failure had also disrupted the sound, and that Amy and the band had been desperate to carry on, but were unable to do so.

Whilst trying to put the pieces of her fractured existence into some semblance of order, Amy began dating a twenty-one-year-old aspiring actor called Josh Bowman. And in typical Amy fashion, it wasn't long before she was shouting from the coconut-treetops that she was free from drugs, and in love again. 'I'm glowing,' she told reporters. 'For the time being I've just forgotten I'm even married. I'm just here on my own, happy and having a good time with Josh. I'll deal with Blake when I get back. Our whole marriage was based on drugs. So being with someone like Josh is much better for me.'

Though frolicking in the Saint Lucia surf with another man whilst still married was hardly becoming behaviour, Mitch and Janis would have no doubt heartily agreed with Amy's comments. After all, they'd strongly objected to Amy marrying Blake in the first place, and then spent much of the ensuing two years pleading with their daughter to leave her miscreant husband. But Blake had also heard about Amy's holiday romance, and rather than wait for her to deal with him on her return as she'd so publicly promised, he instructed his solicitor to commence divorce proceedings on grounds of adultery.

While there is no proof that Blake was responsible, the ink was barely dry on the decree absolute when home videos showing him goading Amy into singing a racist song, and another of her asleep surrounded by assorted drug paraphernalia, surfaced in the media.

But just as the media were beginning to believe they had exacted the last pound of flesh from the couple's tempestuous and oft-troubled relationship, there was to be one last twist in the tale when photos of Amy and the recently-released Blake walking hand-in-hand through Soho were printed in April 2010. Though no ring was evident on Amy's wedding finger, the *Sun* claimed that the couple had gotten engaged again, and were planning to marry in Las Vegas if Amy's US visa application was approved.

♪ ♪ ♪

Though the quickie divorce hadn't cost Amy anything financially, other than the hiring of her own solicitor to ensure the i's and t's were dutifully dotted and crossed on the legal paperwork, her bank balance had taken something of a battering in recent months because of costly tour cancellations, and her regular rehab stints. So to boost her finances she agreed to play a series of lucrative one-off private shows, the first of which came on Friday, 18 December 2010, when she performed at a Russian business tycoon's birthday bash in Moscow and received a reported £1 million for the show. She was flown in on the publicity-shy oligarch's private jet and put up in one of the city's most luxurious hotels. Her performance, on the closed-off top floor of a central Moscow shopping centre, was said to have lasted around forty minutes, and comprised of songs hand-picked by the oligarch.

The following month brought another seven-figure bonanza, with a series of Brazilian shows – including three Summer Soul Festival appearances, the first of which was held at the Stage Music Park in Florianópolis on Saturday, 8 January 2011. Photos taken during the performance show Amy wearing a hip-hugging, low-cut pink gingham dress that left little to the imagination, looking healthier than ever – though her recent boob job undoubtedly helped. Before the show she spent several hours chatting with Rolling Stone Ronnie Wood, who'd apparently spent the New Year in neighbouring Uruguay and had popped across the border to say hello.

Amy is believed to have pocketed another £500,000 from her appearance at the Gulf Bike Week Festival in Dubai the following month – despite being booed offstage. According to the Arab paper *Al Arabiya*, Amy had appeared incoherent and had problems remembering the lyrics. Amy's management issued a statement blaming 'technical issues', particularly with the in-ear system, for Amy's poor performance, but the local production team were said to be disputing the claim. According to other reports, which appeared in the Arab press the following day, many of the 10,000 crowd – having paid Dh300 ($100) a ticket – were considering mounting a campaign to get their money back.

♪ ♪ ♪

In March, the *Daily Telegraph*'s Neil McCormick – who would unknowingly be conducting Amy's last ever interview – was invited along to Abbey Road Studios in St John's Wood, where Amy would be performing the old jazz standard 'Body and Soul' with Tony Bennett for the latter's *Duets II* album, which was set for release later in the year. Though she'd arrived fashionably late, looking edgy and wary of strangers, McCormick could see that Amy had 'filled out since her scrawny drug-addled worst'. Perhaps more importantly, she was sober. It was the first time in a year that Amy had been inside a studio and she was understandably nervous – and not only because of who her singing partner was that day. But the nerves fell away the moment she stepped up to the mic, and watching 'the old veteran and the young

> **'I'm just happy to be here. It's a story to tell my grandchildren, to tell their grandchildren to tell their grandchildren.'**
> **– Amy Winehouse**

ingénue was extraordinary. They stood side-by-side but wrapped their voices around each other, rising and falling, scatting and blending in jazzy cadences.' Like so many others, Bennett was bemused by the juxtaposition of Amy's mature singing voice, reminiscent of Billie Holiday and Dinah Washington in their prime, and her aitch-dropping north London twang. But any misgivings he had about working with her evaporated when Amy mentioned her appreciation for Dinah Washington. And her eyes almost popped out of their sockets when the crooner revealed that he had known Washington personally.

'You're one of my idols,' she gushingly told Bennett during a break in the session. 'I'm just happy to be here. It's a story to tell my grandchildren, to tell their grandchildren to tell their grandchildren.'

♪ ♪ ♪

Though it had taken five long years, Amy had finally amassed enough songs to begin recording her long-awaited third album, and Universal Music Group CEO Lucian Grainge was quoted in the press as saying the new material was 'sounding sensational'.

She also had a new man in her life, thirty-three-year-old film director Reg Traviss, who she'd met in early 2010 through a mutual friend, in the Marylebone pub run by Reg's parents. 'She popped in when I was there one day,' Traviss told the *Times*. 'She walked past and gave me a quick little glance, then she came over and started chatting. One of the people I was with knew her. We hit it off very quickly. What clicked was that we come from similar backgrounds. I'm from Stepney. Amy's family are from

*Amy and boyfriend Reg Traviss attend a party for Universal Music CEO Lucian Grainge in London, June 2010 (left) and (right) Amy during an impromptu performance at London's 100 Club in July 2010.*

Stepney. We liked the same sort of style. I think she understood me from the first time I met her and I understood her.' He was different to all the men that had come and gone from her troubled life, because he was creative in his own right, and didn't need to bask in Amy's reflected glory. 'I've worked with people who are quite high-profile and I've learnt to take people as they are,' he said. 'I don't read the papers.'

'With Reg, I'm the sort of person who will sit down to write and I won't stop until I have an album's worth,' Amy told *Metro*. 'I've needed to have a couple of experiences and so on and Reg is really inspirational. I've just been doing lots of writing recently and Reg is a workaholic. I was speaking to his dad the other day, who said he would come home from work when Reg was a kid and see him writing at the table and then he'd get up for work the next day and Reg would still be writing at the table. So it's really inspirational for me because it gets me doing a lot more. He's looking after me; he's a really good guy. Things are good now. He's a really good influence on me. I'm a lucky girl.'

Traviss was equally enamoured and talked openly about making an honest woman of Amy. 'Amy and I have been talking about getting married, we are looking to book something very soon,' he told the *People* that April. 'I am thinking of getting something sorted in the next six weeks for the end of the year. I love Amy very much; she's a wonderful, talented, lovely girl.'

Amy was also claiming not to have touched drugs for three years, and though she had checked herself out of the Priory Clinic, she was still continuing treatment as an outpatient. With a twelve-date European tour set to commence in the Serbian capital Belgrade on Saturday 18 June, Amy played several low-key warm-up shows, the most notable coming at the 100 Club on Oxford Street, on Sunday 12 June, where she performed in front of friends and family members. The 100 Club, of course, has long been regarded as London's jazz mecca, and so it's somewhat surprising that this was Amy's first appearance at the subterranean venue. Equally surprising, given that she was supposed to have written an album's worth of new material, was that no new songs featured in the seven-song set list.

At long last, it really did seem as though the corner everyone had been hoping Amy would turn was now behind her. To ensure she remained on the straight and narrow whilst away on tour, Raye Cosbert had given strict instructions to the management at each hotel on the itinerary that not only was Amy's room to be searched for alcohol in advance of their arrival, but that its staff were all aware that under no circumstances was she to be served drink. But once again, hope proved to be an illusory chimera, for within the sixth-century settings of the picturesque Kalemegdan Fortress in Belgrade, Amy's frailties were hideously exposed.

The 20,000-strong audience whooped and hollered their appreciation as Amy came out onto the stage in a skimpy, tight-fitting dress, but the cheering soon began to falter as she plonked herself down on the monitor and proceeded to take off her shoes before slumping unceremoniously to the floor. She picked herself up, and after grabbing hold of her bemused bass player as though he was the centre of her gravity, she tottered across to the microphone. The band went into the opening number but it soon became apparent to all that Amy was incapable of providing the accompanying lyric. After mumbling a few incoherent lines whilst hugging herself, seemingly in the hope that it all might just turn out to be a horrible dream, she proceeded to introduce her band – the same band that had been with her for years – yet struggled to remember their names. Having shelled out €38 for the pleasure of seeing Amy up close and personal, the Serbians were less than pleased and, ever so slowly, a crescendo of boos rippled about the ancient citadel. Within a matter of hours, Amy's latest fall from grace had been posted on YouTube for all the world to see.

At first glance, you could be forgiven for thinking the footage is of a comedienne doing an Amy Winehouse skit for television, and it's only when you realise that it's actually Amy that the laughter chokes in the throat. The next tour dates, festivals in Istanbul and Athens, were swiftly cancelled by her management, but within a matter of days the whole tour had been scrapped indefinitely. A spokesperson, who by this time must have felt as though they were reading from a dog-eared script, said that

*Amy hugs herself during her disastrous comeback performance in Belgrade in June 2011 (left) and (right) her last public appearance, onstage with goddaughter Dionne Bromfield at the Roundhouse in Camden, 20 July 2011.*

Amy 'would be given as long as it takes to recover. Everyone involved wishes to do everything they can to help her return to her best.'

On her return to the UK Amy entered the Priory, where she hid away from prying eyes, while Raye Cosbert and the rest of those fighting her corner decided how long a standing count she might need before returning to the ring.

It has since come to light that there were those at Island Records who believed Amy had been unnecessarily pushed into touring. According to the *Independent*, Darcus Beese had thought the decision to send her out on tour was 'mad', and is also believed to have recommended that Amy part company with Raye Cosbert and Metropolis.

Cosbert is repudiating Beese's claims, and is said to be compiling a dossier detailing all the personal support and counselling assistance that Metropolis provided for Amy. These included sorting out the rental agreements on her various homes, sorting out her rehab appointments, as well as providing security in the form of a housemate-cum-minder. A friend of Cosbert's told the same paper, 'It's very hurtful. Raye is currently cataloguing all the help she did receive. Amy always made the decision to play any show, arrangements were always made in discussions with her doctors and really no one could have done more to support her.'

In his article for the *Times*, Nick Godwyn said that he'd found the images from

Belgrade both 'upsetting and strange', and openly questioned Metropolis putting Amy into an environment where she'd be exposed to drugs and alcohol. 'Who knows what the reason was,' he said. 'Maybe her team thought a tour would get her confidence back.'

But in the same piece, he defended her record label bosses, saying they hadn't asked her to do anything since 2007. 'They [Island] had even turned down music, which must have hurt her a lot. She was a lot luckier than some artists who have success in that she wasn't on a treadmill. I know artists who have one day off in a year. Before she got ill, you were lucky if Amy did thirty days in a year.'

Though the dispute is set to continue, it's unlikely that Mitch Winehouse would have remained with Cosbert – who he signed with when launching his own singing career – if he thought him in any way responsible for his daughter's death.

♪ ♪ ♪

Amy's final public appearance was in support of her fifteen-year-old goddaughter Dionne Bromfield at the iTunes Festival – held at the Roundhouse on Chalk Farm Road, on Thursday 21 July – less than forty-eight hours before she was found dead in her Camden home. She'd often said that Dionne had 'more potential than any other girl I've seen', and she was so supportive of her goddaughter's ambitions that she reportedly spent £15,000 on intensive singing lessons for her, and set up her own label – Lioness Records – in early 2009, through which Dionne could release her debut album.

The Roundhouse crowd gave Amy a rousing reception, thinking she was going to perform, but it quickly became apparent that Amy was far from on song. After stumbling about the stage in a somnambulistic stupor, and telling everyone to go out and buy Dionne's debut album, set for imminent release through her Lioness label, she was gone. Not just from the stage, but also from the world's gaze.

The following afternoon Amy met up with her mum Janis and they spent a couple of 'mother and daughter' hours together. Though Amy appeared a bit sluggish, there was nothing in her demeanour to suggest anything was amiss. Janis returned home filled with the maternal glow that all mothers feel after spending some quality time with their offspring, and it was only when the unfolding tragedy reached its apex the following day that Amy's parting words – 'I love you, mum' – took on extraordinary resonance. 'They are the words I will always treasure and always remember her by,' Janis subsequently told OK! magazine. 'She seemed out of it. It still hasn't hit me but I'm glad I saw her when I did.'

Amy returned to the £2.5million Victorian semi in Camden Square that she'd purchased back in 2009, but didn't move into until May, after laying out a further £200,000 for a gym and recording studio to be installed. Later that evening, after receiving her weekly visit from the doctor who her anxious bosses at Island Records had assigned to monitor her health, Amy retired to her bedroom, where she divided her time between chatting on the phone to pals such as Tyler James and Kelly Osbourne, and hammering away on a recently-purchased drum kit. Indeed, such was her enthusiasm that neighbours – thinking Amy was throwing another party, assumed they were in for another sleepless night. 'I was speaking to her last night, she seemed absolutely fine,' a distraught Kelly told *OK!* magazine in August 2011. 'I don't understand how this could have happened.'

The media were equally unsure how it could have happened. 'She was alone, it seems, for the last night of her life,' the *Guardian* reported. 'After seeing a doctor for a routine appointment at around 8:30pm, she played drums and sang into the early hours, until her bouncer [Andrew Morris] told her to keep it down. He heard her footsteps overhead for a while, then it went quiet.'

> **'I was speaking to her last night, she seemed absolutely fine. I don't understand how this could have happened.'**
> **– Kelly Osbourne**

On Saturday morning, Reg Traviss was preparing for the wedding he and Amy were due to attend on Sunday. 'I was calling her but couldn't get hold of her,' he later told the *Sun*. 'I had spoken to her earlier on the Friday night before she went to bed.' He'd planned to spend the night at Amy's house, but after working late, 'I couldn't get hold of her, so I thought she must have fallen asleep'.

Morris – who'd been hired by Metropolis to keep an eye on Amy, as well as keep prying eyes away – checked in on Amy at around 10:00am, but, thinking she was still tired, he left her to sleep in whilst making a mental note to check in again at midday, when breakfast could be served as brunch. He returned to the master bedroom at noon to find Amy still apparently asleep, and, assuming the doctor had perhaps given Amy something to help her rest, went about his daily regime. But as the afternoon ticked by, with no sound emanating from the bedroom, he became increasingly concerned. He went upstairs and knocked on the door, and when no response was forthcoming he entered the room. The first thing that struck him as he approached the bed was that Amy appeared to be in the same foetal position as earlier, the second was that she didn't appear to be breathing. On reaching over to check for a pulse and feeling her cold flesh, he hurriedly grabbed up the phone. In a state of shock, he called for the emergency services. Tragically, it was already too late.

# Epilogue
## All Things Must Pass

**'I see myself making records for ever and ever and ever, until I'm dead.'**

While a senior Scotland Yard detective stood outside Amy's house, rattling off the standard police-procedure patter about how they were continuing with their enquiries into the circumstances of Amy's death, the media circus that had played no small role in this three-part tragedy hurriedly set up stall in Camden Square, and thrust its collective microphone towards anyone who looked like they might have a story to tell.

One story doing the rounds was that Amy had supposedly been seen near her home buying heroin, cocaine and ketamine from a well-known Camden dealer at around 10:30pm the previous evening, and had then embarked on a marathon drug binge that had proved too much for her already ravaged organs. Her spokesman, Chris Goodman, however, was quick to dismiss the rumours, saying, 'At this stage no one knows how she died. There has been speculation that she had taken drugs but we can't say anything until the autopsy. There was no wild party, she died alone in bed. Amy was on her own at home apart from a security guard who we had appointed to help look after her for a couple of years.'

Amy's boyfriend Reg Traviss spoke of his shock and grief, saying that Amy's death had come at a time when she was 'completely normal, happy, healthy, talking about the future'. 'It was like everything stopped,' he said of the moment he heard the news, 'like I'd stepped into another reality – a parallel dimension where everything is the same but something is fundamentally wrong. You are trying to make sense of it. Keeping yourself together because you know now nothing is going to be the same again, ever.'

Reg was also determined to set the record straight about her supposed fatal drugs

*Amy Winehouse photographed in London on 28 April 2008.*

binge, as well as quash rumours about Amy having committed suicide. Accompanying Mitch and Janis on an emotional visit to the rapidly-growing shrine of photos, flowers, and candles outside Amy's home, he told the *Sun* how in recent weeks Amy had been 'full of life, exercising every day and doing yoga'. He went on to say that Amy had been excitedly picking out outfits for a friend's wedding on the Sunday. 'She had laid out her dresses to make up her mind; she was really looking forward to it.'

Clean-cut Reg was the polar opposite of bad boy Blake, and there's no doubting that he loved her dearly. 'She was a brilliant, brilliant laugh,' he said, 'the complete life and soul of everything all the time. She could see situations coming, work someone out the minute they came in the room. She had great comic timing and when someone's as witty as she was, I think that indicates they are quite clever.' What makes the tragedy all the more heart-wrenching is that with Reg, Amy had a real chance of lasting happiness if she could only have kept her promises to keep away

> **'She will be remembered as a world-class icon – as a singer, but also as a personality and as someone who is a real figure of subculture.' – Reg Traviss**

from the drink. Family and friends all saw what a calming influence Reg was on Amy. Reg later told the *Sun* of the normal life the two of them had lived together, saying that the Amy he knew – 'old-fashioned', 'domestic', 'feminine' – wasn't the Amy he'd seen portrayed in media. 'Of all the people I have known, Amy was the most genuine. She lived a very normal life. She was really good to live with. She liked watching TV a lot. She liked to make me something to eat when I got in from work. She liked making food and cooking. That was important to her.'

He also revealed their plans to marry eventually, saying that Amy had discussed it with members of his family. 'I can't describe what I am going through,' he told the *Sun*. 'I want to thank so much all of the people who have paid their respects and who are mourning the loss of Amy, such a beautiful, brilliant person and my dear love. I have lost my darling who I loved very much.'

Reg reflected that, in death, he hoped Amy would achieve the iconic status he felt she deserved, alongside the likes of Marilyn Monroe and Elvis Presley. 'I've thought about Amy's legacy. She used to have a picture of Elvis in her room. She also liked Marilyn.' (Indeed, there are comparisons to be drawn between Amy's death and Marilyn Monroe's last night on earth back in August 1962: both were alone at home with one employee looking after their needs, both had spent the majority of their final evening chatting to friends on the phone.) 'Amy didn't see herself as being in the same category as them,' Reg continued, 'but I personally thought she was in that bracket. She will be remembered as a world-class icon – as a singer, but also as a personality and as someone who is a real figure of subculture.'

*Flowers and tributes left outside Amy's Camden home after her death.*

The press preferred to compare Amy to Janis Joplin, another girl with a voice that belied her years who'd died before her time. Because until 23 July 2011, Janis had been the sole female member of that most exclusive of enclaves within the celebrity cemetery, the fabled 'Club 27'.

Though renowned blues legend Robert Johnson and Rolling Stone Brian Jones had gone before, it wasn't until the toxic trio of Jimi Hendrix, Janis Joplin and Jim Morrison crossed the divide within a ten-month period – between September 1970 and July 1971 – that the legendary club was properly ratified. And though the Grateful Dead's Ron 'Pigpen' McKernan and Badfinger's Pete Ham, both of whom passed away at the age of twenty-seven, would have believed their earthly exploits worthy of a place at the top table, the chair remained empty until Kurt Cobain finally found his nirvana at the end of a shotgun barrel in April 1994. Of course, the club's legion of ghoulish groupies has long proclaimed Richey Edwards to be Club 27's celestial seventh member. But being declared dead isn't quite the same as being confirmed dead, and, while he remains Missing in Action, the Manic Street Preacher will have to settle for honourable membership at best.

♪ ♪ ♪

*Amy's father Mitch, brother Alex, mother Janis, and boyfriend Reg Traviss view the floral tributes left outside her home in Camden Square by fans, 25 July 2011.*

As photographs of Amy stared out from the front pages of newspapers around the world, her adoring public's initial shock quickly turned to anger and frustration. Their frustration was undoubtedly aimed at Amy herself for leaving unannounced, but their anger was directed elsewhere. They had questions that demanded answers, the most fundamental being, why hadn't Amy's management or record label done more to help her?

Following Amy's death, Mötley Crüe's inveterate hellraiser Nikki Sixx told the media that, although he didn't personally know those closest to Amy – her immediate family, management, and record company – he knew that most record labels had 'enablers', whose sole role was to provide artists with everything their heart desired, regardless of the request. 'They just don't want to upset the apple cart, and what happens then is people die. I had so many close calls that I look back on it, why did nobody step up and say, "You know what? If you keep using drugs, we're not gonna release your records. If you keep using drugs, we're not gonna book your tours."'

Russell Brand, who'd suffered similar addiction problems and therefore recognised the symptoms, said in his moving tribute in the *Guardian*: 'When you love someone who suffers from the disease of addiction you await the phone call. There will be a phone call. The sincere hope is that the call will be from the addict themselves, telling you they've had enough, that they're ready to stop, ready to try something new. Of course though, you fear the other call, the sad nocturnal chime from a friend or relative telling you it's too late, she's gone. Frustratingly it's not a call you can ever make, it must be received. It is impossible to intervene.'

While such questions were perhaps understandable given the scant factual information available in the immediate aftermath of Amy's death, just because those closest to her weren't shouting about their efforts from the rooftops, that doesn't mean they were standing idle while she forged a lone furrow on her destructive path. Raye Cosbert and his team had long-since been considered part of Amy's extended family, and would have been beside themselves with worry as lurid tales of Amy's offstage activities slowly overshadowed her talent. And though Island Records' relationship with Amy was first and foremost one of business, they continued to support her long after other labels would have washed their hands.

Amy's family also came in for criticism from the fans, but whilst conspiracy theorists might say that Andrew Morris – who was in the family's employ – had ample time to remove an accusatory suicide note, drug paraphernalia, or any other incriminating evidence from the house before the emergency services arrived, to suggest that her family didn't care is beyond contempt. Indeed, the only criticism that could be remotely directed at Mitch Winehouse – as he himself readily admits – is that he didn't handle the media spotlight as well as he might have done. It's worth remembering that Mitch and Janis were ordinary working-class parents who suddenly found themselves under the media microscope on account of having a supremely talented daughter. And by the time they – and everyone else – became aware of the severity of Amy's drug problems, she would only listen to Blake.

On the Monday following Amy's death, an inquest was opened at St Pancras Coroner's Court. Having listed the deceased's name, date-of-birth, address, marital status, and profession, the coroner's officer Sharon Duff told the two-minute hearing that a 'Section Twenty' post-mortem had been carried out that morning, and that histology and toxicology had subsequently been taken to determine the cause of death. As the scene had been investigated by police and determined non-suspicious, the Assistant Deputy Coroner, Suzanne Greenaway, dutifully adjourned the case until 26 October, issuing interim certificates so that Amy's body could be released to her family for the funeral, which was set for the following day.

Toxicology reports released in August revealed that there were 'no illegal substances' in Amy's body at the time of her death, and that though alcohol was present, it was unclear if it had played a role in her demise. However, when the inquest into Amy's death reopened on 26 October 2011, the coroner finally recorded a verdict of misadventure, after hearing that Amy was five times over the legal drink-drive limit on the night she died and that three empty vodka bottles (two large and one small) had been recovered from her house. The pathologist who conducted her

*Kelly Osbourne and Mitch Winehouse at Amy's funeral on 26 July 2011.*

examination said 350mg of alcohol per 100ml of blood was considered a fatal level; the level of alcohol in Amy's blood was 416mg per 100ml, enough to have stopped her breathing and sent her into a coma.

The court was told that Amy had been drug-free for three years – confirming what her father had previously said – but that she had fallen into a pattern of alternate abstinence and binge drinking. In this instance, she had begun drinking on the night of her appearance onstage at the Roundhouse with goddaughter Dionne Bromfield three days before her death. Her GP, Dr Christina Romete, who had been treating her for several years, said that the night before she died, Amy had told her she did not know if she could stop drinking but that 'she did not want to die'. In a statement issued after the inquest, Amy's family expressed a measure of relief at finally knowing what had happened to her, adding 'Amy was battling hard to conquer her problems with alcohol and it is a source of great pain to us that she could not win in time.'

♩ ♩ ♩

In accordance with Jewish burial tradition, Amy's body would not have been left unattended from the time the body was released from the coroner's court until the funeral and burial; a Shomer, or 'watchman', would have remained constantly with her. In a poignant tribute to Amy, her good friend Catriona Gourlay helped wash

*Reg Traviss (left) and producer Mark Ronson (right) attend Amy's funeral.*

and prepare the body before it was placed in the casket, and made sure Amy's hair was perfectly backcombed and coiffed into her trademark beehive, and that her kohl-black Cleopatra eyeliner was immaculately applied.

Amy's game of Russian roulette had been played out to its grim conclusion, but rather than dwell on the drink and drug demons that had led to her toying with the trigger once too often, Mitch and Janis – who arrived at the Edgwarebury Cemetery in north London in a silver Mercedes with blacked-out windows, with Amy's brother Alex and Reg Traviss – were determined that the day should be a celebration of Amy's life, her spirit, and the prodigious talent that made her the greatest British singer of her generation. Indeed, such was their determination that Mitch ensured there were jokes and laughter alongside the prayers and tears in his moving twenty-minute eulogy. He claimed that Amy had recently completed three weeks of abstinence from alcohol, having told her father, 'Dad, I've had enough of drinking, I can't stand the look on your and the family's faces anymore.' His daughter, he said, was 'the happiest she'd been for years', a fact that comforted the family. 'But knowing she wasn't depressed, knowing she passed away, knowing she passed away happy, it makes us all feel better.'

As he was reading his eulogy, a black butterfly flew into the room, landed on Kelly Osbourne's shoulder, and then fluttered around Mitch. ('Have you ever heard anything like that in your life? It's incredible,' he later said, explaining that he saw the butterfly as a sign sent by Amy; proof that her spirit was with them at the funeral.)

Mitch's eulogy ended with the words: 'Goodnight my Angel, sleep tight. Mummy and Daddy love you ever so much.'

Then, with the poignant strains of Amy's favourite song, Carole King's 'So Far Away' drifting on the sombre air, the 150 mourners – including Raye Cosbert, Island bosses Lucian Grainge and David Joseph, Amy's goddaughter Dionne Bromfield, her stylist Alex Foden, and celebrity pals Mark Ronson, Bryan Adams and Tyler James – said their final goodbyes as Amy's coffin was brought back out into the sunshine for the last time.

Also in attendance were Nick Godwyn and Nick Shymansky, who'd first set Amy on her path. 'There were 300 people at the funeral,' Nick Godwyn said in his *Times* article. 'A lot of them had worked with her. All were distraught. Every person that she met, she touched with either her idiosyncrasies or her talent; her ability to come up with something that would knock you sideways. She was always delivering the unexpected. And she was engaging. Once she had your attention, you didn't walk away.'

> 'When we stepped out of Amy's house at one time, people came up to me and they thanked me for having Amy. That's when I knew, this is something else. To be thanked for giving birth to my child. That's wonderful.' – Janis Winehouse

The cortège then wended its way through the north London streets to the Jewish Cemetery in Golders Green which the Winehouse clan, including Amy, had visited five years earlier to deliver Cynthie's earthly remains to her maker. The nondescript red-bricked building had also served as the last stop-off for a host of famous names, such as Rudyard Kipling, HG Wells, Peter Sellers, Sid James, Keith Moon, Marc Bolan and Cynthie's old flame Ronnie Scott. Following the twenty-minute cremation ceremony, Amy's body was committed to the flames. Her ashes were mixed with those of her cherished nan.

In death as in life, Amy was still front-page news, and while the throng of photographers (with ladders to get the best vantage points) snapped away for all they were worth, friends and family members were handed a photograph of Amy – the same image that had adorned the 'Rehab' remix single just five years earlier. On the back of the photo were details of the Jewish Shiva – the seven-day mourning period of prayer and remembrance which was set to begin within that afternoon at the Schindler Hall in Southgate. Guests mingled around the trestle-tables laden with traditional Jewish fare, but the makeshift bar offering a choice of whisky and sherry remained largely untouched, as if those gathered couldn't bring themselves to imbibe the silent killer that had preyed on Amy from the sidelines while the drugs grabbed all the headlines. Of course, those of Amy's pals who weren't of the Jewish persuasion headed over to Camden to raise a glass or two in the Hawley Arms, where the wake surely went on well into the night.

'In the most tragic of times it was the most wonderful experience that I think I have ever had in my life,' Janis Winehouse later reflected, overwhelmed and comforted by the reaction of Amy's fans. 'When we stepped out of [Amy's] house at one time, people came up to me and they thanked me for having Amy. That's when I knew, this is something else. To be thanked for giving birth to my child. That's wonderful.'

As with every other recording artist gone before their time, Amy's death sparked a renewed interest in her back catalogue. Indeed, within hours of the news being made public, *Back to Black* had topped the iTunes chart, and fans were buying up every available copy of 'Rehab' they could find. This phenomenon has neither rhyme nor reason, as those buying the albums had surely already done so before she passed away. It's as if in doing so they can keep their idol alive.

As we all know, Amy spent many years working on her near-mythical third album, and sources said that the 'sensational' songs Lucian Grainge had alluded to were at demo stage, and that there was 'a lot of material' available. Of course, the final decision as to whether the album sees the light of day rests with Amy's parents, but it's a foregone conclusion that the answer will be in the affirmative. And industry experts are already predicting a huge demand for Amy's posthumous album, and that the – as yet untitled – album will probably outsell *Back to Black*'s ten million copies.

Amy would probably have found it highly amusing that she's set to be even more successful in death. If the lyrics she crafted whilst trawling the depths of the abyss are anything to go by, we can only wonder as to what pitch-perfect missives she might have dispatched from her final odyssey. But, of course, entering the heart of her own darkness was to exact a heavy price. For while she could 'die a hundred times' in song, like the rest of us she was helplessly mortal.

On 14 September 2011 – what would have been Amy's twenty-eighth birthday – the Amy Winehouse Foundation was launched. Established with the goal of supporting charitable activities that provide, in Mitch Winehouse's words, 'help, support or care for young people, especially those who are in need by reason of ill health, disability, financial disadvantage or addiction', the foundation was inspired by Amy's generous and caring nature. Her concern and love for others was, her parents said, a defining part of her personality. 'It is a source of great comfort to know that Amy would be proud of this and right behind it,' said Janis Winehouse, while Mitch reflected, 'Amy touched millions throughout the world and I know she will continue to, though the Foundation.' The Winehouse family were consoled by the thought that Amy's memory would not only be a tragic one – grief could be turned into hope.

When penning his tribute to Amy in the *Guardian*, Russell Brand said, 'She wasn't just some hapless wannabe, another pissed-up nit who was never gonna make it. Nor was she even a ten-a-penny-chanteuse enjoying her fifteen minutes. She was a fucking genius.'

The eminent Swiss psychologist Carl Jung was rather more poetic when describing talents such as Amy. He likened them to the loveliest fruits on the tree of humanity, which hang on the most slender of twigs. And to paraphrase a line from Amy's favourite song, Carole King's 'So Far Away': when Amy fell away from the tree at such a young age, there were so many dreams she had yet to find.

**People**

AMY WINEHOUSE DEAD AT 27

# TALENT AND TRAGEDY

**HER FINAL DAYS**

The singer's anguished life—and why those who loved her could not prevent her tragic death. It was only a matter of time, said her mom

**NME**

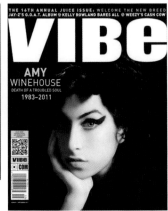

THE 16TH ANNUAL JUICE ISSUE: WELCOME THE NEW BREED
JAY-Z'S G.O.A.T. ALBUM @ KELLY ROWLAND BARES ALL @ WEEZY'S CASH COW

# VIBE

**AMY WINEHOUSE**
DEATH OF A TROUBLED SOUL
1983–2011

VIBE
COM

# AMY WINEHOUSE
## SEPTEMBER 14 1983 – JULY 23 2011

NOW ONLY £1.49

**OK!**

WITH ALL OUR LOVE AND PRAYERS
ISSUE 787 • AUGUST 2 2011 • £1.49 WEEKLY

## THE OFFICIAL TRIBUTE ISSUE

TRAGIC AMY FINALLY AT PEACE R.I.P

• THE FINAL PICTURES
• CELEBRITY TRIBUTES
• HER LAST INTERVIEW WITH OK!

**HER MOTHER'S AGONY**
'SHE TOLD ME "I LOVE YOU"'
THEY'RE THE WORDS I'LL ALWAYS TREASURE'

'BLAKE WANTED HER BACK I'M SCARED HE'LL KILL HIMSELF'

HIS MOTHER'S CHILLING PREDICTION

REMEMBERING AMY WINEHOUSE 1983-2011

**GRAZIA**

£1

NEW PICTURES

**AMY**
## Last hours of the lonely legend

JEN'S SHOCK
AS JUSTIN DEMANDS COUNSELLING

REBOUND!
NOW J-LO'S CHASING A-LIST EX

**100 UNDER £100**
NEW SEASON HITS — IN STORE THIS WEEK!

OPPORTUNITY OVERLOAD
WHY WE'RE THE GENERATION THAT CAN'T DECIDE

**g2**

# AMY WINEHOUSE
1983-2011 By Alexis Petridis

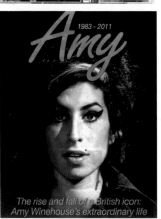

1983 - 2011
## *Amy*

The rise and fall of a British icon: Amy Winehouse's extraordinary life

THE TIMES

# 2
## Tea with Amy

Will Hodgkinson on the Amy Winehouse he met

Plus
Camden Town: inspiration or hell hole?

The curse of 27: the age that claims so many rock lives

**life**
The dilemma of the gay dad
How to come out and

Jewel in the Russian crown
An audience with Mariinsky Ballet star Diana

Sathnam Sanghera
Rhyming slag-off: why are our poets at war?

IN SPECIAL MEMORY OF **AMY WINEHOUSE**

# STYLIST

ISSUE 89
3 AUGUST 2011
STYLIST.CO.UK

'WE ONLY SAID GOODBYE WITH WORDS'

AMY WINEHOUSE 1983-2011

# AMY WINEHOUSE
## 1983–2011

She was brave, beautiful, thrilling and inspirational, a musician whose heartbreaking frankness gave British pop its soul back. Beneath the iconic appearance and troubled self-destroying saga, *Emily MacKay*, a daring talent whose life ended far, far too soon.

*She focused all her force on living out her dreams*

# Amy Winehouse
### September 14 1983 – July 23 2011
## OK! pays tribute to a talented but tragic star

---

Amy Winehouse
## Farewell to lonely legend

As the world continues to mourn the loss of Amy Winehouse, Grazia looks back at her last days and remembers the tiny singer with the huge talent

### Remembering Amy

*A classic songwriter, she took pop in a new direction*

---

## 'SHE WAS THE REAL DEAL'

Amy's unique bohemian iconic, yet her personality always shone through. Here our leading photographers share the stories behind the pictures.

### NO BALL GAMES

## QUEEN OF CAMDEN

North London singer Amy Winehouse's spirit had as much on physical home. As the tragic news broke, Jennie Fullerton headed down to her favourite corners to hear how she lived in Britain.

*'Everyone knew her here'*

## Amy in her words

*"MUSIC IS THE ONLY THING I HAVE WITH REAL DIGNITY IN MY LIFE. THAT'S THE ONE AREA IN MY LIFE WHERE I CAN HOLD MY HEAD UP AND SAY NO ONE CAN TOUCH ME."*

---

## HOW NME FELL FOR AMY

### Influential and unique

*She's fiercely funny and startlingly attractive*

## 'She had so much love to give'

FORMER 'DAILY STAR' COLUMNIST CHARLI MORGAN SHARES HER GRIEF AND MEMORIES OF FRIEND AMY WINEHOUSE

### AMY'S FAMILY AND FRIENDS MOURN THE SINGER

## 'I'm completely devastated'

THOSE CLOSE TO THE LATE SINGER AMY WINEHOUSE TRY TO MAKE SOME SENSE OF HER SUFFERING AND FINAL MOMENTS

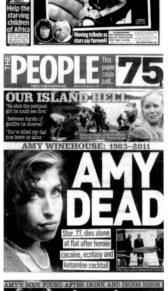

## HEARTBREAK OF FORMER HUBBY AND PALS

# Blake: My tears will never dry

### EX COLLAPSES IN PRISON CELL

SHY SMILE OF MINNIE STAR

2nd mum in Windies

'She knew it was end'

### As a child she was destined to be famous.. but she was reckless and headstrong

# The silencing of a British songbird

One of the most precocious musical talents to emerge in years, Amy Winehouse's private life spiralled out of control and led to a fatal conclusion. **Roya Nikkhah** reports

### Feted as a worldwide star.. but unable to even pick up her five Grammys

'83
'03
'06
'07
'07
'08
'09
'11

She became a mascot for Camden — it is a quieter place today

## Poignant, innovative and human, her best songs are what we will remember

CAMDEN TOWN

### Her love for Blake was total. He was her drug and became all consuming & destructive

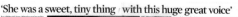

## 'She was a sweet, tiny thing / with this huge great voice'

Hendrix, Joplin, Morrison.. now Amy Winehouse joins the list of rock stars ravaged by drugs

## 'Cause as we kiss goodbye the sun sets, so we are history'

TEARS DRY ON THEIR OWN
BACK TO BLACK (2006)

25.02.11

Amy Winehouse had talent to burn and sang because she had to, says **Alexis Petridis** who remembers an artist whose enormous impact rested on a handful of unforgettable songs

### A losing game

Amy
1983 - 2011

# AMY
# WINEHOUSE

14<sup>th</sup> September 1983 – 23<sup>rd</sup> July 2011

❝ I want to go somewhere where I am stretched
right to my limits and perhaps even beyond.
To sing in lessons without being told to shut up
(provided they are singing lessons). But mostly
I have this dream to be very famous – to work on
stage. It's a lifelong ambition. I want people to hear
my voice and just . . . forget their troubles for five
minutes. I want to be remembered for being
an actress, a singer, for sell-out concerts
and sell-out West End and Broadway shows
– for being just. . . me. ❞ – Amy Winehouse

*Excerpt from Amy's application for the Sylvia Young School*

Published by Plexus Publishing Limited
25 Mallinson Road
London SW11 1BW
www.plexusbooks.com

British Library Cataloguing in Publication Data

O'Shea, Mick.
Amy Winehouse: a losing game.
1. Winehouse, Amy. 2. Women singers–
Great Britain–Biography. 3. Singers–
Great Britain–Biography.
I. Title
782.4'2164'092-dc23

ISBN-13: 978-085965-482-1

Cover Photo by Corbis/ Tim Mosenfelder
Cover and book design by Coco Wake-Porter
Printed in Great Britain by Scotprint

**Acknowledgements**
Professional thanks to Sandra, Laura and Tom
at Plexus UK for their assistance in my bringing
the book in on time, Rupert Tracy, and Jackie and
Richard @ P-PR. Thanks also to Tasha 'Bodacious
Babe' Cowen and Shannon 'Mini-Hepburn' Stanley,
for keeping the tea flowing, and putting up with my
mood-swings and frustrations when occasionally
stumbling over the dreaded writer's block, Paul Young
(not the singer), Lisa 'T-bag' Bird, Johnny Carroll,
Fi Bartlett and the twins, Debbie Mustapha, Zoe
Johnson-Meadows, Martin and Angela Jones, Phil
and Nic Williams. **Mick O'Shea**

Amy Winehouse has given innumerable interviews to
newspapers, magazines, websites, television and radio.
The author and editors would like to give special
thanks to the *Daily Mirror*, the *Sunday Mirror*, the *Daily
Telegraph*, the *Observer*, the *Guardian*, the *Independent*,
the *Sunday Times*, *Metro*, *Harper's Bazaar*, *Totally Jewish*,
*Entertainment Weekly*, *The Word*, *Blues and Soul*, *Blender*,
*Paper*, *New Music Express*, *OK!*, *City Life*, *Scene*, *Stern*,
*Rolling Stone*, *Associated Press*, *The List*, *M*, *Artist Direct*,
*Exclaim* (Canada), *US Weekly*, Accessallareas.net.au,
Daily Mail Online, Times Online, musicOMH.com,
Contactmusic.com, Popjustice.com, nowpublic.com,
Just Drawn That Way, Blabbermouth.net, *Friday Night
with Jonathan Ross*, *The Album Chart Show*, *Breakfast*,
BBC Radio 1.

We would also like to thank Pepe Balderrama
for photo research and the following agencies for
supplying photographs: WireImage/ Mark Allan/
Getty Images; Getty Images/ Samir Hussein; ITV/
Rex Features; AFP/ Getty Images/ Shaun Curry/
Stringer; Richard Young/ Rex Features; WireImage/
Andy Paradise/ Getty Images; Redferns/ Rick
Smee/ Getty Images; Rex Features; Philip Hollis/
Rex Features; John Alex Maguire/Rex Features;
WireImage/Tim Whitby/Getty Images; Redferns/
Rob Verhorst/ Getty Images; Brian Rasic/ Rex
Features; Getty Images/ David Montgomery;
Getty Images/ Mike Marsland; David Butler/ Rex
Features; Getty Images/ Dave Hogan/ Stringer;
Canadian Press/ Rex Features; Frank Doran/ MCP/
Rex Features; Getty Images/ Michael Buckner;
Stephanie Paschal/ Rex Features; Startraks Photo/
Rex Features; FilmMagic/ Sylvia Linares/ Getty
Images; WireImage/ Anthony Harvey/ Getty
Images; FilmMagic/ Jeff Kravitz/ Getty Images;
WireImage/ Hal Horowitz/ Getty Images; Redferns/
Chris Christoforou/ Getty Images; Getty Images/
Scott Gries; Redferns/ JMEnternational/ Getty
Images; Getty Images/ Jo Hale; Getty/ Redferns/
Marc Broussely; Getty/ Chris Jackson; Getty/
FilmMagic/ John Ricard; Getty/ Dave M. Benett;
Getty/ WireImage/ Steve Granitz; Matt Baron/
BEI/ Rex Features; WireImage/ Jon Furniss/ Getty
Images; Getty Images /Dave Hogan/ Stringer;
James McCauley/ Rex Features; WireImage/ Jason
Squires/ Getty Images; Getty Images/ Gareth
Davies/ Stringer; Photofab/Rex Features; Beretta
/ Sims/ Karius/ Rex Features; Getty Images for
MTV; Michael Dunlea/ Rex Features; FilmMagic/
Fred Duval/ Getty Images; Duncan Bryceland/
Rex Features; Getty Images for NARAS/ Peter
Macdiarmid; Getty Images/ Gareth Davies;
WireImage/ Mark Allan/ Getty Images; James
Curley/ Rex Features; Most Wanted/ Rex Features;
KeystoneUSA-ZUMA/ Rex Features; Getty Images/
Dave M. Benett; Mark St George/ Rex Features;
FilmMagic/ Jack/ Getty Images; Getty Images/ Jim
Dyson; Ben Cawthra/ Rex Features; AFP/ Getty
Images/ Ben Stansall/ Stringer; Getty Images/
WireImage/ Mike Marsland.

We would like to thank the following newspapers
and magazines: *People*, *NME*, *Vibe*, *Grazia*, *OK!*, *G2*, the
*Times*, *Stylist*, the *Sun*, the *Daily Mirror*, the *Daily Star*,
the *People*, the *Observer*, the *Guardian*, the *Daily Telegraph*,
the *Independent*.